The Life of Thecla

TOOLS AND TRANSLATIONS

The Westar Tools and Translations series provides critical tools and fresh new translations for research on canonical and non-canonical texts that survive from the earliest periods of the Christian tradition to the Middle Ages. These writings are crucial for determining the complex history of Christian origins. The translations are known as the Scholars Version. Each work, whether a translation or research aid, is accompanied by textual notes, translation notes, cross references, and an index. An extensive introduction also sets out the challenge a text or research aid addresses.

EARLY CHRISTIAN APOCRYPHA

Editorial Board:
TONY BURKE
BRANDON HAWK
JANET SPITTLER

Translations of non-canonical texts out of the Christian tradition are offered as part of the Westar Tools and Translations series in cooperation with the North American Society for the Study of Christian Apocryphal Literature (NASSCAL). The Early Christian Apocrypha series features fresh new translations of major apocryphal texts that survive from the early period of the Christian church. These non-canonical writings are crucial for determining the complex history of Christian origins. The series continues the work of Julian V. Hills, who edited the first six volumes of the series for Polebridge Press. *Studies in Christian Apocrypha* is a subseries to *Early Christian Apocrypha*. The subseries features studies (including short introductions, monographs, and thematic collections of essays) on Christian Apocrypha from any time period and in any of its myriad forms—from early "lost gospel" papyri, through medieval hagiography and sermons incorporating apocryphal traditions, up to modern apocryphal "forgeries."

Volume 1: *The Acts of Andrew*
Volume 2: *The Epistle of the Apostles*
Volume 3: *The Acts of Thomas*
Volume 4: *The Acts of Peter*
Volume 5: *Didache*
Volume 6: *The Acts of John*
Volume 7: *The Protevangelium of James*
Volume 8: *The Gospel of Pseudo-Matthew and the Nativity of the Virgin*
Volume 9: *The Apocryphal Gospels: Jesus Traditions Outside the Bible*
Volume 10: *The Doctrine of Addai and the Letters of Jesus and Abgar*
Volume 11: *The Life of Thecla*

The Life of Thecla

Apocryphal Expansion in Late Antiquity

Andrew S. Jacobs

 CASCADE *Books* • Eugene, Oregon

THE LIFE OF THECLA
Apocryphal Expansion in Late Antiquity

Early Christian Apocrypha 11
Westar Tools and Translations

Copyright © 2024 Andrew S. Jacobs. All rights reserved. Except for brief quotations in critical publications or reviews, no part of this book may be reproduced in any manner without prior written permission from the publisher. Write: Permissions, Wipf and Stock Publishers, 199 W. 8th Ave., Suite 3, Eugene, OR 97401.

Cascade Books
An Imprint of Wipf and Stock Publishers
199 W. 8th Ave., Suite 3
Eugene, OR 97401

www.wipfandstock.com

PAPERBACK ISBN: 978-1-6667-4640-2
HARDCOVER ISBN: 978-1-6667-4641-9
EBOOK ISBN: 978-1-6667-4642-6

Cataloguing-in-Publication data:

Names: Jacobs, Andrew S.

Title: The life of Thecla : apocryphal expansion in late antiquity / Andrew S. Jacobs.

Description: Eugene, OR: Cascade Books, 2024. | Westar Tools and Translations: Early Christian Apocrypha 11. | Includes bibliographical references and index.

Identifiers: ISBN 978-1-6667-4640-2 (paperback). | ISBN 978-1-6667-4641-9 (hardcover). | ISBN 978-1-6667-4642-6 (ebook).

Subjects: LCSH: LSCH: Thecla, Saint—Legends. | Christian women saints—Legends. | Women in Christianity—History—Early church, ca. 30–600. | Christian hagiography.

Classification: BR1720.T33 J21 2024 (paperback). | BR1720 (ebook).

VERSION NUMBER 05/30/24

Scripture quotations marked (NRSV) are taken from the New Revised Standard Version Bible, copyright © 1989 National Council of the Churches of Christ in the United States of America. Used by permission. All rights reserved worldwide.

For my teachers, Susan Ashbrook Harvey
and Elizabeth A. Clark

Contents

Acknowledgments | ix
List of Abbreviations | x

Introduction | 1
The Life of Thecla | 41

Bibliography | 93
Index of Ancient Sources | 99

Acknowledgments

Many thanks to Tony Burke, Brandon Hawk, and Janet Spittler, the editors of Early Christian Apocrypha, for seeing my translation of the *Life of Thecla* online and inviting me to publish a more polished version in their series with introduction and annotations; additional thanks to Cascade Books for agreeing to let me keep that original translation online while creating this fuller (and more accurate!) version for print. Janet Spittler also read through my revised translation with keen and careful eyes, and I am enormously grateful for her suggestions and comments. I originally read portions of this text with students in my Advanced Greek seminar at Harvard Divinity School during the teeth of the coronavirus pandemic, over lively Zoom sessions, and I am grateful for their enthusiasm for Christian apocrypha. The introduction benefited enormously from the collective wisdom of the Boston Area Patristics Group (*Patristica Bostoniensia*) whose diligent and insightful members read it in draft form.

Andrew S. Jacobs
Cambridge, Massachusetts
Fall 2023

Abbreviations

Ancient

Acts John	*Acts of John*
Acts Paul	*Acts of Paul*
Acts Pet.	*Acts of Peter*
Acts Pet. Paul	*Acts of the Holy Apostles Peter and Paul*
Acts Thec.	*Acts of Thecla*

Egeria
    Itin.   *Itinerarium*

Epiphanius
    Pan.   *Panarion*

Eusebius
    Mart. Pal.   *De martyribus Palaestinae*
    Praep. ev.   *Praeparatio evangelica*

Evagrius
    Hist. eccl.   *Ecclesiastical History*

Gregory of Nazianzus
    Ep.   *Epistulae*
    Or.   *Orations*

Gregory of Nyssa
    In cant.   *In Canticum canticorum*
    Vita Mac.   *De vita Macrinae*

ABBREVIATIONS

Hippolytus
    In cant.   *In Canticum canticorum*

Homer
    Il.   *Iliad*

Jerome
    Vir. ill.   *De viris illustribus*

Photius
    Bibl.   *Bibliotheca*

Pseudo-Clement
    Hom.   *Homilies*

Severus of Antioch
    Hom.   *Homilia cathedralis*

Tertullian
    Bapt.   *De baptismo*

Themistus
    Or.   *Orations*

Theodoret
    Hist. rel.   *Religious History*

Modern

AnBoll	*Analecta Bollandiana*
Aug	*Augustinianum*
FC	Fathers of the Church
JBL	*Journal of Biblical Literature*
JECS	*Journal of Early Christian Studies*
JFSR	*Journal of Feminist Studies in Religion*
LNTS	Library of New Testament Studies
MAMA	*Monumenta Asiae Minoris Antiqua*, 1928–1993

ABBREVIATIONS

NHMS	Nag Hammadi and Manichean Studies
NPNF²	Nicene and Post-Nicene Fathers, second series
OECS	Oxford Early Christian Studies, Series 2
PG	*Patroligia Graeca.* Edited by Jacques-Paul Migne. 162 vols. Paris, 1857–1886
PGL	*Patristic Greek Lexicon.* Edited by Geoffrey W. H. Lampe. Oxford: Clarendon, 2004
PO	Patrologia Orientalis
TLL	*Thesaurus Linguae Latinae*
VC	*Vigiliae Christianae*
VCSup	Vigiliae Christianae Supplements
WGRW	Writings from the Greco-Roman World
WUNT	Wissenschaftliche Untersuchungen zum Neuen Testament

Introduction

Thecla in Late Antiquity

In the fifth century CE, in a corner of the Roman Empire subject to so much disruption from local outlaws that troops were stationed on the roadways, pilgrims streamed into a shrine outside of the city of Seleucia (modern Silifke, on the southern coast of Turkey), seeking the healing power of the saint who resided there: Thecla. They came from across the Roman Empire, and even from outside its borders: men, women, children, free, enslaved, Christian, pagan, elite, and uneducated alike. They all sought the undeniable power of the saint: a heroic virgin from apostolic times.

Thecla was one of the most popular Christian saints in late antiquity.[1] Venerated as an apostle and martyr, Thecla was remembered as a wealthy young woman who, upon being converted to a life of celibacy by the apostle Paul, survived multiple condemnations to death and went on to preach on her own. We know about Thecla from several written and non-written sources, most importantly the second-century *Acts of Thecla* (often included as part of the longer *Acts of Paul*) and her later saint's shrine, Hagia Thekla, established in the fourth century near the city of Seleucia.[2] She also appears in late ancient sermons, wall art, pilgrimage flasks, lesser shrines (notably in Rome and Egypt), and numerous literary references and adaptations.[3] Thecla's origins are mysterious: some scholars have claimed her story was based

---

1. The literature on Thecla is enormous. For a recent overview, see Kraemer, "Thecla."

2. On the textual history of the *Acts of Thecla*, including its relationship to the longer *Acts of Paul*, see Barrier, *Acts of Paul and Thecla*; and Barrier, "Paul and Thecla, Acts of." On Hagia Thekla, see Dagron, *Vie et miracles*, 55–79; Davis, *Cult of Saint Thecla*, 36–80; and Kristensen, "Landscape, Space, and Presence."

3. On Thecla's shrines and pilgrimage flasks, see Davis, *Cult of Saint Thecla*. Some prominent material remains are cataloged by Naureth and Warns, *Thekla*. On literary influence, see Dabiri and Ruani, *Thecla and Medieval Sainthood*.

The Life of Thecla

on oral traditions later incorporated into the *Acts of Paul*, but the source of those purported oral traditions is unclear. Thecla's appeal is widespread and undeniable: Christians for centuries turned to her as a powerful saint and intercessor, one step removed from the apostle Paul.[4]

The *Life and Miracles of Thecla* is a fifth-century text that draws on and illuminates Thecla's place in the late ancient Christian world. The *Life*, which I translate in this volume, explicitly follows the narrative structure of the earlier *Acts*. The *Miracles*, which have been translated into English by both Linda Ann Honey and Scott Fitzgerald Johnson, are by the same author and recount forty-six miracles performed (mostly posthumously) by Thecla from Hagia Thekla.[5] The two parts were composed as a literary diptych (like the Gospel of Luke and Acts of the Apostles, to which the author refers in the *Life*'s preface), but the *Life* also circulated independently.[6] While the *Acts* was enormously popular in late antiquity and the Middle Ages, and is well known to modern readers, the *Life and Miracles of Thecla* are less well known. Yet this lesser-known fifth-century expansion of a famous apocryphal text deserves our attention for several reasons.

First, the *Life of Thecla* provides precious information about how the story of Thecla was received and imagined at the site of her ongoing veneration. How did her devotees understand, interpret, and perhaps even transform the well-known story of a rich, beautiful girl who gave it all up to become Christ's apostle? Second, the *Life* opens up a window into the ways apostolic stories continued to be written and rewritten throughout late antiquity, blurring the line between neat scholarly genres like *apocrypha* and *hagiography*. Finally, the *Life* participates in a movement of late ancient authors creatively rewriting "classical" and "biblical" texts in new literary styles.[7]

---

4. Most scholars agree that Thecla is not a historical figure, or at least cannot be affirmed as historical beyond her literary life in the *Acts of Paul* and later texts. As Ross Shepard Kraemer notes, "Modern scholars give no historical credence to its portrait of a female disciple of Paul in the mid-first century" ("Thecla," 488). See also Barrier, *Acts of Paul and Thecla*, 10–12. For a counterargument on Thecla's historicity, see Honey, "Thekla," 96–105.

5. Honey, "Thekla," 362–439; Johnson, "Miracles of Saint Thekla" (which also includes facing Greek text from Dagron's critical edition).

6. See Dagron, *Vie et miracles*, 141–47 (of the 12 extant manuscripts Dagron examined, four contain the *Life* and *Miracles* while eight contain just the *Life*).

7. Johnson (*Life and Miracles*, 67–112) analyzes the text in the broader context of "ancient paraphrase," such as the Empress Eudoxia's biblical poems created out of patchwork lines of Homer or the recondite poetic "paraphrase" of the Gospel of John by Nonnus of Panopolis, both also from the fifth century.

Introduction

The *Acts of Paul and Thecla*

The *Acts of Thecla* was the central section of a longer *Acts of Paul*, although there is evidence that the *Acts* was read on its own in late antiquity and may even have been composed earlier and incorporated later into the *Acts of Paul*.[8] Written in Greek, it probably originated in the second half of the second century.[9] Like other contemporary "apocryphal acts of the apostles," the *Acts* centers on the disruptive effects of an apostle preaching the merits of celibacy and the appeal of the apostle's anti-marriage message to women.[10] In several such stories, married women abandon their prominent husbands to embrace celibacy and follow the apostle; the ensuing conflict between abandoned husband and homewrecking apostle frequently ends in the apostle's execution and martyrdom. The *Acts* is a variation on this narrative: Thecla is not yet married (although she is engaged) and the apostle Paul is not condemned to death but Thecla, the girl who embraces virginity, is subject twice to unsuccessful public execution (earning her the later sobriquet "protomartyr").[11]

Since the *Life* explicitly follows the narrative structure of the *Acts*, it is worth rehearsing its outline here briefly.[12] *Acts* begins with Paul and two duplicitous companions, Demas and Hermogenes, arriving in Iconium where they are welcomed by an Iconian named Onesiphorus (1–4).[13] While Paul preaches on the holiness of chastity and virginity, Thecla, listening from a window next door, overhears him and is converted to a life of chastity (5–7). She rejects her fiancé, Thamyris, and the pleading of her

---

8. See Barrier, *Acts of Paul and Thecla*, 21–24.

9. Barrier (*Acts of Paul and Thecla*, 23–24) suggests "the last 30–40 years of the second century."

10. Key works on this issue include Davies, *Revolt of the Widows*; Burrus, *Chastity as Autonomy*; and Cooper, *Virgin and the Bride*, 45–67.

11. The longer *Acts of Paul*, in which the *Acts of Thecla* are usually embedded, does end with the apostle's martyrdom in Rome: on legends of Paul's death, see Eastman, *Ancient Martyrdom Accounts*.

12. Paragraph numbers are taken from the English translation of J.K. Elliott, *Apocryphal New Testament*, 364–72. In more recent translations of the *Acts of Paul*, the verse numbers are presented as: 1–25=Acts Paul 3:1–25; 26–43=Acts Paul 4:1–18.

13. All three of these names appear in Pauline and pseudo-Pauline letters (Col 4:14; Phlmn 1:24; 2 Tim 1:6, 1:15, 4:19), leading to a rich scholarly discussion about the relationship between the *Acts* and other Pauline traditions. See, as a start, MacDonald, *Legend*; and Hylen, *Modest Apostle*.

The Life of Thecla

mother, Theocleia, to turn away from Paul and back to Thamyris.[14] Enraged, Thamyris has Paul arrested; Thecla sneaks out of her house and visits Paul in jail (8–19). While Paul is punished with flogging and expulsion from Iconium, Thecla is condemned to execution by burning (19–21). A miraculous hailstorm douses the fire, and she leaves Iconium to search for Paul, finding him outside of Iconium praying for her. She pleads for baptism and offers to cut her hair and follow him. Paul defers her baptism but allows her to accompany him on his journey (22–25).

They arrive at Antioch where almost immediately Thecla is sexually assaulted by a prominent local leader, Alexander. She publicly humiliates him and is arrested and sentenced to death (26–27). Paul, who claims not to know Thecla, disappears. Entrusted to a relative of the emperor, Tryphaena, Thecla prays for the salvation of Tryphaena's dead daughter (28). Thecla is condemned to the beasts; in the arena, a lioness fights to protect Thecla but is killed (29–33). Alexander devises more punishments for Thecla, but she escapes harm. Thecla baptizes herself in a pool of man-eating seals and is protected by a divine flash of lightning. When Tryphaena faints and is thought to be dead, the proconsul halts the execution (34–36). Thecla is freed and given money and enslaved servants by Tryphaena (39). Thecla finds Paul once more and, after announcing her baptism and conveying some of Tryphaena's wealth to Paul, she goes off to evangelize (40–41). She goes first to Iconium where she speaks briefly with her mother and then heads off to Seleucia. The oldest version of the *Acts* ends with a short notice of Thecla's death (42–43).

The simple two-act structure is repetitive but effective. Thecla's character is vivid and her adventures gripping. As scholars have pointed out, the basic structure of the *Acts*, like many of the so-called apocryphal acts, echoes contemporaneous ancient Greek novels which recount the adventures of a beautiful young couple who fall in love and must navigate extraordinary hazards (shipwrecks, bandits, executions, enslavements) before coming together at the end to marry.[15] While the *Acts* subverts

---

14. As Dagron (*Vie et miracles*, 175 n. 9) points out, "Thecla" is usually understood as a "diminutive" of "Theocleia," although he floats the provocative idea that "on pourrait imaginer qu'au contraire Théokleia soit une forme développée, imaginée à partir d'un nom indigéne, Thékla" (one could imagine that, on the contrary, Theocleia is a developed form, imagined from an indigenous name, Thecla).

15. Discussion in Perkins, *Suffering Self*; Cooper, *Virgin and the Bride*; Barrier, *Acts of Paul and Thecla*, 1–10; and Burrus, "Mimicking Virgins." Thomas, *Acts of Peter*, places Apocryphal Acts in the wider contexts of ancient novelistic literature (including biblical

Introduction

this narrative—the "happy ending" is not marriage and reproduction but celibacy and religious devotion—it uses similar narrative techniques, including the hint of erotic attachment between Paul and Thecla, who becomes enraptured at the sound of his voice. This tangled engagement with "secular" literary tropes and themes will continue in later adaptations and expansions of Thecla's story, including the *Life of Thecla*.

Later Texts and Art Featuring Thecla

The *Acts of Thecla* was enormously popular.[16] Dozens of manuscripts survive in the original Greek along with translations into every language of the late ancient world.[17] Tertullian, writing in North Africa in the late second or early third century, is our first external witness to the popularity of the text. Tertullian decried Christians who looked to Thecla as precedent for women baptizers: he reports that the *Acta Pauli* on which they rely was only recently composed by a presbyter in Asia Minor and therefore lacks apostolic authority (*Bapt.* 17).[18] In the late fourth century, Jerome was aware of the *Journeys of Paul and Thecla* (Περίοδοι Pauli et Theclae); he mentions the text in his catalog of Christian authors and deems it "apocrypha," citing Tertullian's earlier condemnation (*Vir. ill.* 7, his chapter on Luke). Around the same time, a western pilgrim named Egeria traveled to Seleucia and Thecla's shrine and heard "all the *Acts of Thecla* read" there (*Itin.* 23.5). Epiphanius of Cyprus, a noted heresiologist, even cites one of Paul's ascetic "beatitudes" from the *Acts* as simply a saying of the apostle.[19] Today, asking whether or not the *Acts* was considered "canonical" or "authoritative" misses the point: it was *read* and was a persistent and popular part of Christian culture throughout this period. A recent volume on *Thecla and Medieval Sainthood* shows how influential the text was as a blueprint for saints' stories from Ireland to Armenia.[20]

---

texts like Esther and Daniel).

16. For an overview of "culture-making" through literary and material memorializations of Thecla in late antiquity see Castelli, *Martyrdom and Memory*, 134–71.

17. Many of them are described in Kaestli and Rordorf, "La fin de la vie de Thècle."

18. Barrier ("Cainite Invocation") places this brief notice in the context of Tertullian's larger, possibly anti-gnostic arguments.

19. Epiphanius, *Pan.* 77.27.7: "Blessed are they that keep pure the flesh" (*Acts Thec.* 5).

20. Dabiri and Ruani, *Thecla and Medieval Sainthood*.

The Life of Thecla

Thecla became an influential figure apart from the specific narrative of the *Acts*. In the late third century, ascetically-minded bishop Methodius of Olympus composed his *Symposium*, a riff on Plato's famous dialogue that swaps out pederastic Athenian men at a drinking party for Christian virgins in a serene garden; their host, Aretē (Virtue), calls upon the ten virgins to extol "chastity" (ἁγνεία, *hagneia*). Thecla delivers the eighth of ten speeches (adding to her praise of virginity an anti-astrological defense of human free will) and, at the conclusion, is given the crown of victory by Aretē and pronounced "chief" (πρώτη, *prōtē*) among the symposiasts.[21] By the late fourth century Thecla's popularity as a virgin worthy of emulation was widespread. She appears in the texts of prominent bishops: Gregory of Nazianzus (*Or.* 21, in praise of Athanasius), Gregory of Nyssa (*In cant.* 14), and Epiphanius of Cyprus (*Pan.* 78.16.7, 79.5.2), to name a few.[22] We also encounter evidence of women named for Thecla (a name otherwise unattested before the *Acts*), including a martyr remembered by Eusebius of Caesarea (*Mart. Pal.* 10–11, 20), a correspondent of Gregory of Nazianzus (*Ep.* 56, 57, 222, 223), and the saintly ascetic Macrina, who was given the name of Thecla in secret by her mother while she was still in the womb (Gregory of Nyssa, *Vita Mac.* 3.2).[23] A fifth- or sixth-century homily mistakenly ascribed to John Chrysostom attests to the establishment of Thecla's feast day, which was eventually commemorated in late September.[24] The Ps.-Chrysostom homily begins with an invocation of Thecla's "image," probably a literal reference to a saintly portrait placed before the congregation.[25] Indeed it is precisely during this same period that Thecla materializes into the physical landscape of a newly Christian empire. In addition to multiple sites of veneration (see below), she also appears in art and mobile objects: wall paintings in Italy, Asia Minor, and Egypt; pilgrimage flasks

21. For more on this text and its philosophical context see Burns, "Astrological Determinism" and Lavalle Norman, *Aesthetics of Hope*.

22. For more citations see Hayne, "Thecla and the Church Fathers"; and Hylen, "'Domestication' of Saint Thecla," 6.

23. On "namesakes" of Thecla in the Egyptian papyrological record, see Davis, *Cult of Saint Thecla*, 201–208. The *Miracles* also mentions a woman named Thecla, whose mother was "still pagan" but whose son, Aurelios, is cured of scrofula by the saint (*Miracle* 11). Either we are to assume the woman's father was Christian or that "Thecla" was a popular regional name regardless of religious affiliation.

24. English translation in MacDonald and Scrimgeour, "Pseudo-Chrysostom's Panegyric to Thecla," 154–57.

25. MacDonald and Scrimgeour, "Pseudo-Chrysostom's Panegyric to Thecla," 157–59.

Introduction

traveling across the empire from various shrines; even small objects like combs, boxes, and medallions feature Thecla in recognizable scenes from the *Acts*.[26] As the "cult of the saints" ramped up in the Christian Roman Empire, Thecla, the virgin-martyr-apostle, led the way.

Veneration of Thecla

Multiple sites for the veneration of Saint Thecla emerged in the fourth through sixth centuries across the late ancient world. A basilica in Milan was dedicated to Saint Thecla in the fourth or fifth century.[27] A church in Rome claimed to have relics of Thecla by the seventh century, substantiated by a later, long ending of the *Acts* in which the virgin, in her old age, longs once more to see Paul and seeks him out in Rome (see my summary and discussion below).[28] No clever hagiographical expansion explains the prominence of Thecla's veneration in Egypt, in conjunction with the popular Saint Menas, although Stephen Davis has outlined the extensive material and literary evidence for her veneration there.[29]

The most famous of these sites of veneration was Hagia Thekla ("Saint Thekla"), on the southeastern coast of Asia Minor just outside the city of Seleucia, where the *Acts* places the end of Thecla's life. Whether Thecla was already connected with Seleucia when the *Acts* was composed or its composition inspired veneration there is unknown. By the late fourth century it was the preeminent site for veneration of the saint.[30] In the 370s, Gregory of Nazianzus secluded himself at the "convent (παρθενῶνα, *parthenōna*) of the holy virgin Thecla" to avoid episcopal ordination (*De vita sua* 549). When Egeria visited a decade later there was a "church of the martyrium" alongside "many monasteries" housing "as many men as women" (*Itin.*

---

26. See Naeurth and Warns, *Thekla*, 93–99 for a catalog of Thecla images (some of which are reproduced in plates at the end of the volume) and the plates, with discussions, in Davis, *Cult of Saint Thecla*. Pillinger ("Thekla in the Cave of St. Paul") compares an ancient fresco of Thecla, Paul, and Theocleia uncovered in a cave in Ephesus in the 1990s with other contemporary (fifth-century) material representations of the saint.

27. Krautheimer, *Three Christian Capitals*, 74–77.

28. Translated by Elliott, *Apocryphal New Testament*, 372; see also Kaestli and Rordorf, "La fin de la vie de Thècle," 90–93; and Rordorf, "Saint Thècle," 79–81.

29. Davis, *Cult of Saint Thecla*, 83–194.

30. See Hill, *Early Byzantine Churches*, 208–17 for an attempt to reconstruct the earliest, fourth-century buildings at the site, including their appearance during the period the *Life and Miracles* were written.

23.4–6). Egeria also points out the shrine's remote and precarious location, noting the "huge wall" that protects the martyrium from Isaurian bandits. In the fifth century, Theodoret of Cyrus tells of two Syrian monastic women who spent decades wearing chains, enclosed in a cell, leaving only to make pilgrimage to Jerusalem and to "the shrine of the triumphant Thecla in Isauria": "they journeyed both there and back without food," a journey of at least two weeks (*Hist. rel.* 29.7; trans. Price).

Our richest literary source for the activities at Hagia Thekla is the *Life and Miracles of Thecla*, which were produced by an insider to the shrine who worked and preached there (on the author, see below). The second half of the diptych, the *Miracles*, covers events that take place mostly over the fourth and fifth centuries and gives readers insight into the architecture, politics, and appeal of the saint's healing shrine. Not long after the *Life and Miracles* were written, the site was expanded. While in temporary exile from Constantinople in the 470s, Emperor Zeno supposedly had a vision of "the holy, greatly tried protomartyr Thecla" who promised him the restoration of his imperial throne. Once successful, Zeno—who was himself Isaurian—"dedicated a huge sanctuary of outstanding magnificence and beauty to the protomartyr Thecla" (Evagrius, *Hist. eccl.* 3.8; trans. Whitby). Archaeological work conducted in the early 1900s shows that the expansion continued into the sixth century: three basilicas (one of which is probably the one built by Zeno), baths, a shrine in a cave, and other structures testify to the site's "rapidly growing pilgrimage clientele."[31] The *Miracles* make clear that Thecla appealed to all kinds of Christians, and not a few pagans, who made pilgrimage to her shrine: men, women, lay people, monastics, of all classes and geographic origins. Her appeal by these later centuries vastly outstripped her narrow portrayal as a fervent ascetic in the *Acts*. Stephen Davis justly proclaims, "In the early Christian period, Thecla was venerated as the most popular female saint after the Virgin Mary."[32]

---

31. Davis, *Cult of Saint Thecla*, 39. Dagron (*Vie et miracles*, 59–63) summarizes the partial excavations, reported in Herzfeld and Guyer, *Meriamlik und Korykos*. Hill (*Early Byzantine Churches*, 217–34) surveys the remains that might plausibly be attributed to Zeno, with helpful comments on Herzfeld and Guyer's reports.

32. Davis, "Thecla," 6661.

Introduction

Overview of the *Life of Thecla*

It is into this world, permeated with texts, images, and shrines to Thecla, that our anonymous author ventured to make his own distinctive literary contribution. This recondite literary diptych is a valuable window into the reception of a saint and her *Acts*. The *Miracles* have received more modern attention than the *Life* (even though more copies of the *Life* survive), precisely because they introduce us to real people involved with Thecla's cult site at Hagia Thekla, as well as ecclesiastical intrigues, and political jostling among Christians on the fringes of the Roman Empire.[33] The *Life* gives us access to a different kind of religious world: the cultural imaginary in which classical tales of apostolic wonder are reframed into "higher" literature for (one presumes) a more sophisticated audience of devotees.

Author and Date of Composition

Until Byzantinist Gilbert Dagron put together a critical edition of the *Life and Miracles* in the 1970s, modern readers, relying on a deficient seventeenth-century edition, accepted the attribution found in manuscripts: Basil of Seleucia, bishop of the city from the 430s or 440s until the late 460s.[34] This misattribution may have been due to a mention in the late ninth-century *Bibliotheca* of Photius, who noted that Basil "extended the deeds, contests, and victories of the protomartyr Thecla into verses" (*Bibl.* cod. 168).[35] Of course, it would make sense that a well-educated local bishop would produce a document meant to promote the jewel of his See (even though the *Life and Miracles* are patently not in verse). Dagron's restoration of the full text of the *Life and Miracles* quickly corrected this misattribution. Key chapters from the *Miracles* missing from the early modern edition made clear not only that Basil was not the author but that the author and Basil were bitter enemies.[36] In *Miracle* 12 the author recounts three miracles Saint Thecla performed for him, including a reversal

---

33. Davis, *Cult of Saint Thecla*; and Johnson, *Life and Miracles*.

34. Dagron, *Vie et miracles*, 16. Basil was a prominent figure at several fifth-century ecumenical councils: see Wuk, "Pragmatic Necessity."

35. Cited in Dagron, "L'auteur," 7.

36. Kateusz (*Mary and Early Christian Women*, 60–63) argues that the *Life* is "much older" than the fifth century, but her arguments do not take into account the content of the *Life and Miracles* that places the composition squarely in the fifth century, such as discussion of Basil as the author's contemporary.

of his excommunication at the hands of "this youngster Basil (how he became bishop and seized control of the church, unworthy as he is, even of the stage, I will leave aside for now)" (trans. Honey).[37] The contretemps with Basil probably occurred after the composition of the *Life*, which we can possibly place in the 440s; the composition of the *Miracles* continued for much longer, perhaps into the late 460s or early 470s (as the end of the *Miracles* excoriates Basil's episcopal successor, Porphyrius).[38] Since the author does not seem aware of Zeno's expansion of the shrine in the late 470s, we can assume he was finished before then.

Despite providing no name for himself in the text, the author is a lively presence in the text, telling us everything but his name. In fact, his authorial presence is *so* lively that it is hard to disentangle his careful self-presentation from the other highly literary and stylized qualities of the work. Byzantinist Derek Krueger, in a study of ascetic authorship, remarks of the *Life*: "The performance of authorship on display here is in part an elaborate act of self-positioning, using various textual strategies to negotiate the writer's standing both among his literary peers and within the church."[39] These twin contexts—"his literary peers" and "the church"—frame what the author chooses to reveal about himself.

In the preface and concluding section of the *Life*, the author describes some of the circumstances in which he came to write this work. It is, first and foremost, the "fulfillment of a vow" to Thecla. Indeed, in the *Miracles* the saint seems personally invested in the completion of the work, appearing directly to the author when his enthusiasm for the endeavor is waning to indicate her approbation and delight at the writing project (*Miracle* 31). In the preface to the *Life*, he also attributes his work to the urging of "a pious man" (v. 3) and "the best of men—I mean Achaius, the best and wisest of all" (v. 9). Achaius would presumably be known to the author's local Seleucian audience; we may infer that he was a man of some importance whose imprimatur would give the work added prestige. In the conclusion to the *Life* the author once more refers to Achaius (unnamed

---

37. Dagron ("L'auteur," 9) notes that the term Honey translates as "youngster," μειράκιον (*meirakion*), should be understood as an insult rather than an indication of actual age difference; we might translate it as "whippersnapper" (Krueger, *Writing and Holiness*, 88, opts for "pipsqueak").

38. See Dagron, *Vie et miracles*, 17–19; the author was active at Hagia Thekla during four episcopal reigns (of Dexianus, John, Basil, and Porphyrius) spanning the 430–470s, although he may not have begun his composition until the 440s.

39. Krueger, *Writing and Holiness*, 79.

INTRODUCTION

but called here "the one who ordered me") and additionally calls him "the holy man who is your [Thecla's] ward" (28.8) The author uses this term "ward" (τρόφιμος, *trophimos*) in two other places: to describe Thecla's relationship to her enslaved caretakers (*Life* 10.3) and to describe a young man who was healed by the saint despite his grandmother's pagan unbelief (*Miracle* 11). Is Achaius a patron of the shrine who has benefited from Thecla's healing? If so, it is strange that the author does not include this event among the dozens of miracles in the second part of his work. Given the long period over which our author labored on the text (as he tells us and as is evident from editorial insertions in the *Miracles*), we might guess that Achaius was an early patron whose influence faded over time, making his inclusion in the *Miracles* either unnecessary or unwise.[40]

The early prominence and later disappearance of Achaius (Thecla's "ward" and "the best and wisest" of men) highlights a major feature of the author's "self-presentation" that Krueger points to in his analysis: his desire to embed himself among both the religious elites of Seleucia and the literary elites of his region and the challenges he faces in doing so. Krueger writes: "While the author classes himself among Thecla's devotees, he also displays his eagerness to class himself as one of the regional literati."[41] The author refers to and cites classical authors (Thucydides, Herodotus, Homer), and numbers himself among the "literati" (ἐλλόγιμοι, *ellogimoi*); he refers modestly to his literary project in his preface, but also assures his readers he has the skills necessary to avoid "archaic" or overly stuffy prose.

Toward the end of the *Miracles*, the author introduces a set of miracles that took place "among the wise men and literati" (σοφοῖς τε καὶ ἐλλογίμοις, *sophois te kai ellogimois*) (*Miracle* 37): "grammarians" (*Miracle* 38) and "sophists" (*Miracles* 39–40), all of whom are pagan but nonetheless receive the saint's beneficence. The author then includes himself as the culmination of this set of "literati" miracles while also tying his oratorical skills to his prominence at Thecla's shrine. He refers to a time he was slated to deliver a

---

40. Dagron (*Vie et miracles*, 21) remarks: "présent dans l'introduction et la conclusion de la *Vie*, il disparaît tout à fait des *Miracles*" (present in the introduction and conclusion of the *Life*, he disappears completely from the *Miracles*). Achaius appears with a more elaborate biography ("a nobleman [ἰλλούστριον, *illoustrion*], learned philosopher, and Christian man") in a later iconophile text loosely based on the *Life and Miracles* called "the achievements of the holy apostle and protomartyr Thecla in Myrtle Wood," which I discuss below.

41. Krueger, *Writing and Holiness*, 82; on the classical background of the author, see Narro, "La scontro tra formazione classica."

brief public speech for the saint's day although "I was not yet one of those who speak in churches" (*Miracle* 41; trans. Honey).[42] He credits Thecla with his success as a speaker ("the Martyr extended her hand and grace to me in such a way that I even seemed to be somehow noteworthy"). Soon after, we learn, the author "was deemed worthy of the clerical council and the register of preachers and priests," and boasts that Thecla "was beside me much of the time," even acting as his assistant during late nights of oratorical composition. Perhaps this escalation in rank signals another, unspoken motive for his undertaking the *Life and Miracles*: to prove his mettle as an orator at the shrine and earn his rank as "preacher and priest."

The author also depicts his success as an orator and cleric as volatile and even controversial. I have already mentioned his conflict with the bishop, Basil, who "for no reason" excommunicated the author for three days (the author's reinstatement is one of the miracles he ascribes to Thecla). He apparently got along with Basil's two predecessors, Dexianus and John (see *Miracles* 7–8 and 44); he battled publicly with Basil (*Miracle* 12); and in the epilogue of the *Miracles* he prays for Thecla's aid against "that dog, that ferocious swine, that base and perverse Porpyhrius," the new bishop who has, apparently, forbidden the author from preaching in the saint's church.[43] The author's life, as he gives us glimpses of it in the *Miracles* especially, toggles between miraculous success and unearned calamity—much like his saintly patron, Thecla.

These biographical revelations lead Dagron to describe our author as "a quite odd writer" (un bien étrange écrivain).[44] His writing style, particularly in the *Life*, is ebulliently literary: he luxuriates in long sentences (which I have, on occasion, broken up grammatically and typographically), fulsome descriptions, and self-conscious references to his literary models (particularly the *Acts*). Much like his carefully constructed persona, poised rockily between "literary peers" and "the church," his lifelong literary endeavor is informed by lofty rhetorical and theological aims.

---

42. The author was suffering from a debilitating earache which the saint healed in time for him to deliver his speech.

43. Dagron (*Vie et miracles*, 16) calls this plea to Thecla "mi-pathétique, mi-délirant" (half-pathetic, half-delusional).

44. Dagron, "L'auteur," 6.

INTRODUCTION

Outline of the *Life*

As noted above, and as the author explicitly notes himself, the outline of the *Life* closely follows that of the *Acts*, with some deletions and insertions throughout that do not disrupt the general narrative flow. Chapter numbers follow Dagron's critical edition.

Preface. Circumstances of composition. The author notes his impetus for writing (his vow and the urging of Achaius), disclaims any attempts to "one-up" the existing *Acts*, and notes his insertion of speeches to give the account an "old-fashioned beauty."

1. *Thecla hears Paul's preaching.* The author omits the *Acts'* description of Paul's arrival at Iconium and his welcome by Onesiphorus on the road. Instead, after a brief summary of Christ's ministry and the mission of the apostles, the author introduces us to Thecla and to Paul, who is in the midst of preaching in Onesiphorus's house next door to Thecla.

2. *Paul's preaching.* This first invented speech is a vastly expanded version of Paul's ascetic beatitudes in the *Acts*; while Paul still praises purity he also leaves room for the equal "blessedness" of marriage.

3. *Thecla rejects her family.* Thecla's changed demeanor draws her mother Theocleia's prurient suspicions; Theocleia summons Thecla's fiancé, Thamyris, and delivers a speech pleading for his aid in averting shame for both of their families.

4. *Thamyris pleads with Thecla.* Thamyris delivers a long speech praising their forthcoming union, warning of the perils of a bad reputation, and even suggesting they consummate their marriage immediately. When Thecla refuses to listen, the entire house goes into mourning.

5. *Thamyris meets Paul's false friends.* Here we first meet Demas and Hermogenes, who pretend to be Paul's companions but are filled with venom against him. They encounter the enraged Thamyris and explain the depravity of Paul's preaching against marriage and his rejection of true "resurrection" (reproduction through children).

6. *Paul's arrest.* At dawn, Thamyris seizes Paul with a mob force and delivers a long praise of family and a denunciation of Paul before the proconsul; Demas and Hermogenes remind him to also level the accusation of Paul being a Christian.

7. *Paul's apologia.* Paul condemns the immorality of polytheism (its myths and rituals) and contrasts them with the moral transformation that Christ has brought through chastity and virginity, while still leaving room for morality in marriage.

8. *Thecla visits Paul in jail.* Thecla bribes her way out of her house and into the jail to see Paul.

9. *Paul's teaching.* Paul warns Thecla of the many ways that the devil will seek to derail her from her path to salvation.

10. *Paul and Thecla on trial.* Thecla is discovered missing by her enslaved servants and found with Paul by Thamyris; they are both brought before the proconsul Cestillius, who has Paul whipped and expelled from Iconium.

11. *Thecla's trial.* Cestillius exhorts Thecla to choose marriage and family.

12. *Thecla's first martyrdom.* Thecla keeps silent, and Theocleia denounces her in a short speech. Wood is gathered to burn her alive. Thecla thinks she sees Paul in the stands (although it is Christ in Paul's shape) and delivers a speech to him begging for his help. She forms herself into the shape of a cross, steps into the flames, and is saved by a miraculous storm.

13. *Thecla reunited with Paul.* Paul is praying and fasting near the town with Onesiphorus and his family; Thecla encounters Onesiphorus's hungry children seeking food. Once reunited, Thecla and Paul each deliver a speech of thanks to God.

14. *Thecla requests baptism.* Thecla and Paul engage in a dialogue in which she requests baptism and he defers her request until later, fearing a second conflict that will be worse than the first.

15. *Confrontation with Alexander in Antioch.* When Thecla and Paul are approaching Syrian Antioch, the mere sight of Thecla in the distance enflames a local leader, Alexander, who then assaults Thecla. When she defends herself, and delivers an outraged speech of accusation, Alexander is humiliated. The author notes that a shrine stands today at the gates of Antioch commemorating that event.

16. *Thecla entrusted to Tryphaena.* Thecla is handed over for judgment and entrusted to Tryphaena, a relative of the emperor whose daughter has recently died. Alexander subjects Thecla to a parade of the animals who will be sent against her in the arena, but the meanest lioness surprises everyone by acting submissive to Thecla.

17. *Thecla intercedes for Falconilla.* Tryphaena's late daughter Falconilla appears to Tryphaena in the night begging for Thecla's intercession. Tryphaena then delivers a plea to Thecla who in turn prays to Christ for intercession.

Introduction

18. *Thecla's second martyrdom.* Tryphaena delivers a long lament (in two parts) over Thecla when Alexander arrives to take her to the arena for execution by the beasts. Thecla prays to God, not for her own freedom, but for recompense for Tryphaena.

19. *Thecla faces the beasts.* Thecla is at first defended by the lioness, who dies in a fight with a lion. The women in the stands are divided in their desire for Thecla's death and sympathy for her plight.

20. *Thecla baptizes herself.* Thecla prays to Christ before leaping into a pool of man-eating beasts. She assumes she will be killed and achieve baptism by blood (martyrdom), but a heavenly fire kills the seals and forms a wall protecting Thecla from public view.

21. *Tryphaena swoons.* The women of the crowd pacify the remaining animals with fragrant perfumes that are vaporized in the miraculous fire. Alexander devises another means of execution which also fails; Tryphaena, overcome with distress, swoons and is taken for dead. Alexander, fearful, pleads with the governor to end the spectacle and free Thecla.

22. *Miracles versus magic.* An excursus on the difference between miracles, which are God's work in the world, and magic, which is the sinister work of evildoers. Pagans often mistake the former for the latter. The narrator celebrates biblical wonderworkers and then Thecla delivers a speech of defense before the governor.

23. *Thecla freed.* The governor frees Thecla, who delivers a speech of thanks to the governor and to God. The governor then delivers a lengthy praise of Thecla.

24. *Thecla and Tryphaena reunited.* Thecla returns to Tryphaena's house; Tryphaena delivers a speech of thanks for Thecla and makes Thecla her heir in place of Falconilla. Thecla converts Tryphaena's household.

25. *Thecla and Paul reunited.* Thecla sets out in "manly garb" to search for Paul; she finds Paul in Myra and explains (in indirect speech) everything that happened in Antioch.

26. *Thecla rejoices with Paul.* Thecla delivers a long speech detailing all of the theological and moral instruction she has received from Paul. Paul delivers a speech in praise of Thecla; she then leaves to return to Iconium.

27. *Thecla returns to Iconium and then goes to Seleucia.* Thecla goes to Onesiphorus's house and delivers a speech praising God. She meets briefly with her mother and then goes to Seleucia. The author provides a long description and praise of the city.

28. *The end of Thecla's life*. Thecla performs many miracles in Seleucia; at the end of her life, she does not die but sinks into the earth at the site where her altar stands today. The author delivers thanks to the saint and promises to write a second volume detailing her miracles.

The two-act structure of the *Acts* remains largely intact in the *Life* (chapters 1–4 in Iconium, chapters 15–26 in Antioch), as does the sequence of events, the characters, and the outcomes. The omission of the opening scene of the *Acts*, in which Paul, Demas, and Hermogenes meet Onesiphorus and his family on the road to Iconium, makes sense in the transformation of a "section" of the *Acts of Paul* into a free-standing *Life of Thecla*, as does the inclusion of prefatory and concluding material in the first-person. Similarly, references to a memorial to Thecla in Antioch and an effusive description of Seleucia, with some references to the fifth-century shrine at Hagia Thekla, anchor the *Life* in the contemporary world of saintly veneration. The most significant additions to the narrative are the invented speeches given to major characters and the notice on the end of Thecla's life in the final chapter.

Added Speeches

"By weaving speeches into" the *Life* "where possible," the author announces in his preface, "we have imparted to it (at least I think so) an old-fashioned beauty, while keeping the particular and distinct form of speech for each character" (v. 6). Certainly the most robust contribution the author of the *Life* has made in his revision of the *Acts* are the extended speeches delivered by most of the main characters of the story. We can identify two classical sources for the author's penchant for invented speeches and an additional contemporary Christian resonance.

First, there is the tradition of realistic but invented speeches embedded in classical Greek histories, beginning with Thucydides and Herodotus (both of whom the author mentions in his preface).[45] Historians, especially following Thucydides's example, were often candid that they were not reproducing verbatim speeches delivered by their historical subjects, but careful approximations; readers were therefore conditioned to read historical speeches as containing "elements of fidelity and invention."[46] The author of the *Life* is certainly harkening to this historiographic

45. For a thorough overview, see Marincola, "Speeches in Classical Historiography."
46. Marincola, "Speeches in Classical Historiography," 121.

commonplace, following their lead in saying "a character spoke 'such things' (*toiauta*) rather than 'these things' (*tauta*)."[47] He repeats several times that characters spoke "such things" (see 3.1; 4.1; 10.1; 14.1; 17.1; 18.6; 23.4; 26.25), even flagging the inventedness of the speeches by describing their contents as "likely" (10.1; 20.7). The ascription of long and creative speeches to the characters in the *Life* serves a similar purpose to their role in classical histories: to impart intellectual gravity both to the characters in the story and to the one recounting their story.

The author is also drawing on the classical rhetorical device of *prosopopoeia* (also called *ethopoeia*) or "speech-in-character." "Speech-in-character" was one of the fundamental tools of oratorical instruction in the ancient world (and is, of course, related to the speechifying in histories, as well as the recitation of dramatic and poetical texts). Students would be assigned a character and a situation and told to improvise a speech suitable to that character and his situation.[48] Such an exercise allowed students to practice technical skills, like voice modulation and situational improvisation, while also deriving moral lessons from the (usually dire and dramatic) situations assigned to them. By inventing long, carefully constructed speeches for his characters, the author of the *Life* demonstrates his own skill as a professional rhetor and imparts pathos to his characters.

While the author clearly draws on the classical literary traditions of historical speeches and *prosopopoeia*, we might also hear resonances with Christian liturgical forms that were becoming common during this period. As more preachers (like our author) came from the ranks of men schooled in oratory, they incorporated rhetorical flourishes like *prosopopoeia* into their sermons, speaking in the voices of their biblical subjects. Famous preachers like John Chrysostom frequently spoke "as" biblical characters in the course of their preaching.[49] Basil of Seleucia, our author's onetime nemesis, likewise spoke "as" Jesus and Death in a homily on Lazarus.[50] These homiletic flourishes were connected to another liturgical art form in its infancy during this period: choral compositions performed in the voices of

---

47. Marincola, "Speeches in Classical Historiography," 120.

48. For excellent recent overviews see Muehlberger, *Moment of Reckoning*, 129–39; and Ludlow, *Art, Craft, and Theology*, 119–43.

49. Ludlow, *Art, Craft, and Theology*, 144–81.

50. On this homily see Cunningham, "Basil of Seleucia's Homily." My thanks to Susan Ashbrook Harvey for pointing me to Basil's sermons and reminding me of the homiletic adaptation of *prosopopoeia*.

The Life of Thecla

biblical characters.[51] These were liturgical performances by church choirs in which biblical characters expanded on their scriptural stories; sometimes these choral performances could be antiphonal—that is, different parts of a choir could take up different characters and perform a choral dialogue. This instance of liturgical invented speech appears in the fifth and sixth centuries among Christian communities in the Greek and Syriac East, as well as among Jewish communities in the same areas. It is possible that the invented speeches in the *Life* also invoked this choral liturgical context.[52] The chapters that contain multiple short speeches among multiple characters might have resonated with antiphonal choruses: Paul and Thecla's dialogue in ch. 14 or the sequential short speeches of Falconilla, Tryphaena, and Thecla in ch. 17.[53] The overlap of oratorical and liturgical performance of invented speeches (in speech or song) fits in well with the career of the author, who moved from secular rhetor to "preacher and priest."

The invented speeches also serve a specific literary function: they allow the author to create a tighter link between the *Acts* and the *Life* as, at several places, he incorporates direct quotations from the *Acts* into his invented speeches. At *Life* 12 he incorporates a line from the *Acts* into Theocleia's denunciation of her daughter ("I shall use her very words," 12.4); at *Life* 15 he uses a phrase from the *Acts* in Thecla's denunciation of Alexander ("I could not use more moving words than these phrases of the martyr," 15.15); at *Life* 22, he cites the *Acts* in Thecla's defense before the governor ("it would probably be better to add nothing to the very words the martyr used," 22.16). These direct citations of the *Acts* serve the literary aims of the author in two ways: on the one hand, they reinforce the "historicity" of the original *Acts* and show his reverence for the sacred text (which was, no doubt, frequently read at the shrine and familiar to any potential reader); on the other hand, it highlights his own creativity in the invented speeches, which are both much more elaborate than the speeches in the *Acts* but also

---

51. Cunningham ("Basil of Seleucia's Homily," 162) notes that Basil's prosopopoetic homilies likely influenced the sixth-century choral composer Romanos Melodos.

52. Frank ("Crowds and Collective Affect," 169–70 and nn.1–3) provides useful bibliography on these choral performances and raises a brief comparison with prosopopoetic speeches in late antiquity, as does Lieber ("On the Road"). Brock ("Poetry and Hymnography," 664–65) points out that the Syriac dialogue poems have roots in an older Near Eastern form of "precedence dispute." My thanks to Georgia Frank for discussion of sources on this topic.

53. Honey ("Thekla," 80–87) discusses the description of Thecla as a "chorus-leader" in *Miracle* 44, but sees more significance in choral dancing than singing.

Introduction

(at least from the author's perspective) true to the "voice" of the *Acts*' familiar characters: even as she waxes on for several paragraphs, Thecla sounds like Thecla, to the point where weaving "her very words" into the invented speech demonstrates the author's skill (at least ostensibly).

The author also exercises some creativity as to when and how he endows characters with longer speeches. At times one or two sentences in the *Acts* become longer perorations, as at *Life* 6 (Thamyris's speech at Paul's trial), 11 (Cestillius's and Theocleia's speeches at Thecla's execution), and 23 (the proconsul's praise of Thecla at her release). At other times the instance of direct speech is preserved but its meaning altered, as when the opening of the plea of Tryphaena's late daughter Falconilla is not about her mother receiving Thecla but about her mother's "pointless" mourning (*Life* 17). The author has also added speeches where the *Acts* records no direct speech from the characters: Paul preaches about the devil's wiles to Thecla in prison (9), and Thecla delivers a prayer before her second martyrdom (20) and a long doxology on Paul's teachings afterward (26). Predictably the apostle and his protégée receive the most additional opportunities at speech, allowing the *Life* to "update" their highly ascetic and somewhat antisocial teachings into something more suitable for the fifth century (see below on Themes in the *Life*).

At other times where we might expect an expanded speech, even minimal direct speech is removed, most notably at Thecla's final meeting with her mother during her brief return to Iconium. In the *Acts* the heroine delivers a final plea to Theocleia: "Theocleia, my mother, can you believe that the Lord lives in heaven? For if you desire wealth the Lord will give it to you through me; or if you desire your child, behold, I am standing beside you" (*Acts* 43; trans. Elliott). The *Life* instead reports that, upon arriving in Iconium, "she avoided her mother and family and even her home" (27.1) to deliver a long speech in Onesiphorus's house and then (in indirect speech) "discussed a few things with her mother Theocleia about faith and conduct according to Christ" (27.7). It's difficult to speculate on creative choices an author has *not* made, but it is at least clear that he preferred to expend his oratorical and compositional skills on expanding the Christian teachings coming from Thecla rather than to resolve any lingering narrative tensions in Thecla's story.

The Life of Thecla

The End of Thecla's Life

The *Life*'s other major addition to the *Acts* is the extended account of Thecla's journey to Seleucia and the end of her life. In what seems to be the earliest version of the *Acts*, Thecla visits Iconium one last time, implores her mother to convert, and "having thus testified, she went to Seleucia and enlightened many by the word of God; then she rested in a glorious sleep" (*Acts* 43; trans. Elliott).[54] In the *Life*, the author provides an extended description of Seleucia, from the rushing down of the mighty river Calycadnus to the excellence of its inhabitants, second to nearby Tarsus only in that Tarsus "is the homeland and city of Paul, from whom it became possible for us to have the holy virgin" (*Life* 27.11). The speech in praise of a city was a staple of classical rhetoric of the high empire (the so-called Second Sophistic), and the author's short panegyric of Seleucia thus functions as a small oratorical showpiece in addition to a species of local boosterism.[55] This chapter also provides a segue to the *Miracles*, recounting (in brief) Thecla's settlement on the cliffs outside the city (the future site of Hagia Thekla) from which she ousted the "demons" Sarpedon and Athena (the first two of the *Miracles* recounted in the second half of the literary diptych).

After summarizing Thecla's apostolic activities in Seleucia (preaching, catechizing, baptizing, performing miracles) the author then informs us that Thecla "by no means died": rather, the ground opened up beneath her and "she sank down while still living and went down into the earth" (*Life* 28.2). This indication that Thecla neither died nor left human remains (relics) seems to find its first expression here in the *Life*, no doubt reflecting common understanding of the functioning of the shrine of Hagia Thekla (where Thecla still "lived," under the site of the altar) and its lack of visible relics from the saint. Later "long endings" of the *Acts* expand upon the idea of Thecla passing into living rock.[56] In two "long endings," Thecla's escape into the rocks is precipitated by threats to her virginity (echoing her trials in the two halves of the *Acts*, in Iconium and Antioch). In the shorter "long ending," Thecla escapes "into the rock alive" and travels underground to Rome in search of Paul; finding he has died,

---

54. See the discussion in Kaestli and Rordorf, "La fin de la vie de Thècle."

55. Kensky ("Ephesus") argues that the roughly contemporaneous *Acts of Timothy* circulated in part to promote religious travel to Ephesus.

56. For a full collection of extended endings of the *Acts*, see Kaestli and Rordorf, "La fin de la vie de Thècle." The shorter long ending (Thecla in Rome) is text VII in their collection (pp. 90–92); the longer long ending is text III (pp. 41–46).

she "rested in a glorious sleep" and is interred in a church near Paul (presumably the site of her Roman cult). In the longer "long ending," Thecla has been living in a "cave" near Seleucia, teaching and healing; when, later on, her virginity is threatened by drunk intruders, she prays to God and is provided an opening in the wall of the cave into which she enters; the wall seals up behind her leaving only a trace of her garment.

As Dagron details in his introduction to the critical edition, these "long endings" of the *Acts* make the most sense as amplifications or even rivals of the early tradition witnessed by the end of the *Life*. The Roman ending merely extends Thecla's journey away from Seleucia to a new location while the longer ending places Thecla's shrine in a cave corresponding to the placement of the altar after the rebuilding of the Hagia Thekla later in the fifth century under Zeno.[57] Both add the repeated element of sexual assault found in the *Acts* to create a three-act, rather than two-act, drama: Iconium to Antioch to Seleucia. The question remains, then: if the *Life* is the first witness to this dramatic non-death end of Thecla's life, what is its origin? It is, of course, impossible to know for sure but it does seem the author of the *Life* is mediating a local tradition for a wider audience. By early the next century the tradition of Thecla "living" in the rock below her shrine had spread: Severus of Antioch, bishop from 512–518, delivered a sermon on Thecla's saint day in which he remarked that, while her soul made its way to heaven at the end of her life, "her body was deposited in the earth and to this day it is hidden in the holy and glorious temple and it enacts those things which are characteristic of Thecla, that is, healings and miracles" (*Hom.* 97).[58] Preaching just a generation or so after the composition of the *Life and Miracles*, the bishop of Antioch takes as a given that the unseen body of Thecla remains interred at her shrine, the source of the endless flow of miracles there.

Themes in the *Life*

In addition to having a strong aesthetic style, characterized by elevated prose and invented speeches for the main characters, the *Life* presents a consistent

---

57. Dagron, *Vie et miracles*, 47–53; see also Kaestli and Rordorf, "La fin de la vie de Thècle," 27–37.

58. Severus's homilies only survive in Syriac translations; for discussion of this homily in the context of Thecla's Syriac legacy, see Burris, "Reception of the Acts of Thecla," 77–85.

set of themes. While the themes I elucidate below are present, to some extent, in the older *Acts*, they are also transmuted to make sense for a fifth-century audience. We might compare various adaptations of Jane Austen novels into modern films. To be sure, some of Austen's original interest in the lives of young women embedded in complex social structures remains, but the attention to gender, class, and (in some recent adaptations) race modifies these stories for the concerns of a newer audience. Much as Austen adaptations occasionally rile the Regency author's modern audiences, we might also imagine that the *Life*'s amplifications, modulations, and alterations to the themes of the *Acts* might have similarly offended "fans" of Thecla. Nevertheless, we should also probably assume that the particular themes that become the focus of the *Life* spoke to the ways Thecla's story was being received and interpreted centuries after it began circulating.

Thecla as "Girl," Virgin, Martyr, Apostle, and "Stranger"

At the center of the *Life* is the character of Thecla who transforms over the course of the story from "girl" to "martyr and apostle." Thecla is called "girl" (κόρη, *korē*) more than two dozen times in the *Life*: by the narrator, by herself, by various men and women talking to and about her. By contrast, the *Acts* never uses this word to describe its heroine. While the Greek word *korē* is often translated somewhat archaically as "maiden," it carries the same resonances as our modern, English word "girl": a child rather than a woman, from whom we would not have expectations of adult maturity or behavior. That it is a *girl* doing all that Thecla does—leaving home, risking her life, defying the sexual desires of various aristocratic males—is portrayed as all the more astounding and, indeed, miraculous. After Thecla survives her second martyrdom and delivers a speech, the author recounts: "When the martyr said these things, the governor was amazed at the intensity and manliness of the girl, and at the dignified and philosophical tenor of her words" (*Life* 23.1). Thecla's "girlishness" is not unproblematic: after escaping her first martyrdom and reuniting with Paul outside Iconium, she acknowledges the difficulties of an attractive "girl" traveling along with an older man. She offers: "I shall follow you, after cutting off most of this girlish and misleading hair, so we'll readily be able to avoid onlookers who meddle in such matters. This altered form, I think, will overshadow what you call my beauty and attractiveness" (*Life* 14.3). Just because Thecla is a "girl," an unmarried minor, does not make her physically secure in a world in which freeborn men claimed casual sexual access to unprotected persons of lower status: women, girls, boys, and men, both free and enslaved.

The sexual dangers faced by Thecla are emphasized over and over throughout the *Life* as the narrator and characters refer to Thecla as "virgin" (παρθένος, *parthenos*) almost as much as they call her "girl." Both terms designate Thecla as unmarried, although "virgin" is more specific in marking her sexual inexperience. More than that, however, "virgin" functions as something of an honorific for Thecla throughout the *Life*: she is not just a virgin but "the virgin," a title that signals her special, almost unique, devotion to the message of purity that Paul delivered to the Iconians.[59] Thecla is handed over to Tryphaena's custody as she awaits execution in Antioch specifically because she has requested from the judge a guardian to protect her virgin status from the rapacious Alexander: "For as unconcerned as she was with cowardice when it came to the dangers, so much was she concerned with the safety of her virginity" (*Life* 16.2). Though Thecla's final speech to Paul recounts the finer points of Trinitarian Christology that she claims to have learned from him, she (and we) hear him preach almost entirely about virginity and purity in Iconium; it is for this preaching that he is whipped and expelled from the city and for which Thecla's own mother demands her execution (as in the *Acts*). Thamyris's long praise of family and reproduction during the trial is opposed not only by Paul's speech of defense but by Thecla's mute, virgin body. Long after Paul has left the story, that virgin body remains front and center.

"Virgin" is part of a trio of titles with which the narrator addresses Thecla in his closing chapter: "O virgin and martyr and apostle" (28.8).[60] That she is a martyr is perhaps contestable on technical grounds as she is condemned to death twice but cannot be killed; ancient audiences of Thecla's story were uninterested in such technicalities, however. In the opening chapters of the *Life*, martyrs play a key role in the founding of the faith: "the many and countless flocks of martyrs sprouted up and rained down after Christ's own ascent into heaven. This, in turn, was the time when Thecla lived, not after lots of other men and women martyrs but she was the second one immediately after the apostles and Stephen the martyr (whom the word of truth acknowledged as first), the first among women" (*Life* 1.2–3). The luster of martyrs and martyrdom had by no means faded

---

59. *Life* 1 does refer to "the holy Virgin Mary" (1.2) in a creedal summary of Christ's life, but otherwise "the virgin" is used only of Thecla.

60. See Honey, "Thekla," 69–75.

The Life of Thecla

away from the institutionalized and imperialized Christianity of the fifth century. To the contrary, martyrologies became deeply embedded in the liturgical and material life of the Christian Roman Empire. Thecla's story was recited alongside that of other heroes of the faith who were remembered as sacrificing their lives for Christ. Elizabeth Castelli singles out the *Life* as a crucial late ancient memorial in which "Thecla comes to be produced as the quintessential figure of the woman martyr."[61]

The author also praises Thecla as an apostle in his preface and closing chapter;[62] he may be the first Christian writer to do so. At some points in their transmission histories, titles were added to the *Acts* and Ps.-Chrysostom's homily that refer to Thecla as "protomartyr and apostle," but it is the author of the *Life* who first calls her "apostle" in the body of his text.[63] What's more, he consistently uses a masculine form of the noun with a feminine form of the article, a grammatical feat possible in ancient Greek: Thecla is ἡ (feminine) ἀπόστολος (masculine) (*hē apostolos*), which we might translate as "the she-apostle." Other ancient Greek nouns occasionally alter their gender by use of the feminine article: "human" (ἄνθρωπος, *anthrōpos*), "god" (θεός, *theos*), and "teacher" (διδάσκαλος, *didaskalos*) are some common examples. Paul in his letter to the Romans famously refers to Phoebe as a διάκονος (*diakonos*, "deacon" or "minister") another grammatically masculine title that could become gender-variant (Rom 16:1).[64] The author of the *Life and Miracles* is innovating only insofar as no one had, to that point, described someone as a "she-apostle," an honor that seems to remain unique to Thecla

---

61. Castelli (*Martyrdom and Memory*, 137; see also. p. 151), points out that the *Life* "commemorates Thecla as a 'martyr' in a way that [the *Acts*] never came close to achieving." Although the *Life* does not use the term, by the sixth century the term *protomartyr*, used of Stephen in the fourth century, was also being applied to Thecla.

62. Dagron notes that at least one manuscript omits "and apostle" in the triad of "virgin, martyr, and apostle" in *Life* 28; it does, however, appear in the epilogue of the *Miracles* (Dagron, *Vie et miracles*, 408). In addition, the author refers to Paul and Thecla as τὸν ἀπόστολον (*ton apostolon*) and τὴν ἀπόστολον (*tēn apostolon*) in *Miracles* 4 (Dagron, *Vie et miracles*, 294).

63. *PGL* 211 notes the *Acts* and Ps.-Chrysostom homily alongside the *Life* in its subentry III.D, "of Thecla" under ἀπόστολος.

64. In this case the gender variance is signaled by a feminine participle, οὖσαν (*ousan*, "[she] who is"). In the same chapter Paul also includes women and men together under masculine titles; as is standard in ancient Greek, mixed-gender groups like this take a masculine article: so Prisca and Aquila are "[masculine] co-workers" (Rom 16:3) and Andronicus and Junia are "[masculine] kinsfolk and fellow-prisoners . . . pre-eminent among the apostles" (Rom 16:7).

well into the Middle Ages.⁶⁵ As an apostle, she does what other first-century apostles did: she preaches, teaches, and baptizes. Our fifth-century author does not portray this behavior as problematic even though he lived in a time when Christian women may have taught, rarely preached, and probably never baptized. As I discuss below, gender, sex, and sexuality are complicated in the *Life* but it's possible that by ascribing this special title to Thecla, "the she-apostle," the author is actually making clear that what Thecla did in the first century is in no way possible for women centuries later. As "first martyr" and "apostle," Thecla stands alone.⁶⁶

Thecla's apostolic uniqueness is signaled by another title she claims later in the *Life*: "stranger." The author takes this sobriquet directly from the *Acts*, even directly citing one of Thecla's more famous lines verbatim: "Do not force the stranger (ξένη, *xenē*)!" (*Acts* 26; *Life* 15.14) In the extended version of this speech (defending herself from Alexander of Antioch's sexual assault) Thecla describes herself as "stranger" twice; she also describes herself as a "stranger" in her defense before the Antiochene governor (*Life* 22.14). As in the *Acts*, the term is also used first of Paul by his detractors (twice in the *Acts*, nine times in the *Life*).⁶⁷ He is derided as a "stranger, a swindler, and drifter," a "stranger and vagrant," a "stranger and old man" (*Life* 3.13; 4.4, 5; 11.12). The role of "stranger" complements the office of "apostle," literally "someone sent away": to be an apostle (like Paul, and then Thecla) is to be the stranger saying and doing "strange things" in unknown parts of the world to spread God's word. For this reason, Thecla settles in neither Iconium nor Antioch, but in Seleucia, far

---

65. Mariamne, the sister of Philip in the fourth-century *Acts of Philip*, is included among "the apostles" twice with Philip and Bartholomew (8:21; 9:1). In her chapter on "Woman Apostles: Preaches and Baptizers," Kateusz (*Mary and Early Christian Women*, 40–65) includes Mariamne and Thecla alongside Irene of Macedonia and Nino of Georgia as women called "apostles." The narratives of Irene and Nino are later texts (and survive only in Syriac and Old Georgian respectively), although Kateusz argues they are all evidence of very early traditions of women baptizing and being known as "apostles."

66. Mary Magdalene is first called "apostle to the apostles" along with Martha and Eve in the third century by Hippolytus, *In cant.* 25 (although these passages do not survive in Greek: see text and translation in Smith, "Hippolytus' Commentary," 361), but the idea of Magdalene as *apostolorum apostola* ("apostle to the apostles") because she is the first to find the empty tomb becomes common in the medieval West (see Jansen, "Maria Magdalena," 61).

67. Paul also adopts the term for himself in Iconium when he calls himself a "strange preacher" who will say "strange and incredible things" (*Life* 2.2).

from home, where she will remain the "stranger-apostle" even centuries after her body disappears into the ground.[68]

Gender, Sex, Sexuality, and Society

Thecla's "strangeness" shapes other major themes of the *Life* that are adapted from the *Acts*. We have already seen how Thecla's status as a "girl" and vocation as a "virgin" set her apart and confound those whom she encounters. Her anomalous nature in the *Life* allows Thecla to operate outside the traditional structuring systems of gender and sexuality while leaving them in place for everyone else. Thecla as a "virgin and apostle and martyr" may challenge sexual systems but the broader theological narrative in which she is embedded ultimately reins in and tamps down such challenges for the *Life*'s late ancient readers.

We see this reining in present in one of the most famous scenes in both the *Acts* and the *Life*: Thecla's offer to cut her hair in order to follow Paul. In *Acts* 25, when Thecla finds Paul after escaping her near-martyrdom in Iconium, she proclaims to him: "I shall cut my hair and follow you wherever you go!"[69] After some hesitation on Paul's part he lets her accompany him to Antioch, where Alexander the Syrian "desired her when he saw her." Rosie Andrious and others have argued that Thecla's promise to cut her hair was unfulfilled, as immediately after Alexander still found her sexually desirable: "The narrative logic demonstrates that Thecla must have retained her long hair because she continues to look beautiful."[70] Nevertheless this promise to "cut [her] hair," read in conjunction with a later detail that Thecla was "wearing a mantle that she had altered so as to make a man's cloak" when seeking Paul a second time (*Acts* 40), has led some historians to see Thecla as the

---

68. Only once is she identified as a "stranger" in the second part of the *Life and Miracles* (*Miracle* 2). *Xenē* can also mean "pilgrim" in this period; perhaps the author wishes to affiliate Thecla more closely with the throngs of pilgrims who come to visit her shrine during his time. On pilgrimage to Hagia Thekla, see Davis, *Cult of Saint Thecla*, 64–73.

69. The word used for "I shall cut my hair," περικαροῦμαι (*perikaroumai*), seems to appear nowhere else in extant ancient Greek in this form. *LBG* even suggests it be translated "ganz benommen sein" (to be completely dazed), from a different Greek root. Nonetheless the hair-cutting translation remains standard and, as we see from the *Life*, must have been how it was understood in late antiquity as well.

70. Andrious, *Thecla*, 69–74, cited at 73; see similarly Van Pelt, "Thecla," 201.

predecessor to hagiographic tales of later "cross-dressing" saints: Christians assigned female sex at birth who lived as male ascetics.[71]

Julie Van Pelt, however, has argued that the Thecla of the *Acts* was not a model for later stories of saints living as men; rather, Thecla was retroactively understood as disguising her gender by the author of the *Life* (perhaps even influenced by early versions of those cross-dressing saints' lives). Whereas it's possible to read Thecla's offer to cut her hair as hypothetical or conditional in the *Acts*, the *Life* is unequivocal both in the rationale for the hair-cutting and its actuality.[72] Thecla offers: "I shall follow you, after cutting off most of this girlish and misleading hair, so we'll readily be able to avoid onlookers who meddle in such matters. This altered form, I think, will overshadow what you call my beauty and attractiveness" (*Life* 14.2). Thecla is clear that the haircutting is meant to alter her beauty and disguise her "girlish" appearance. When they arrive at Antioch and Alexander offers Paul gifts and money for Thecla, "Paul denied that the woman belonged to him in any way whatsoever—*if indeed it were possible to know for sure that she was a woman*" (*Life* 15.8, emphasis added). Van Pelt notes that this additional phrase about Thecla's uncertain gender "provides an interpretation of the scene in the [*Acts*] that aligns Thecla with transvestite saints: it suggests that she did indeed cut off her hair, with the purpose of disguising herself for safe travel."[73] Rather than the ambiguous reading of *Acts* inspiring later hagiography, then, it was the *Life* that introduced a reading of Thecla as gender-bending and cross-dressing.

The *Life*'s clarity on Thecla's gender disguise, however, also underscores its ineffectiveness since (as in the *Acts*) Thecla's disguise in the *Life* does not deter Alexander's sexual assault. In fact, all of Thecla's attempts to disguise her beauty and her gender fail. Toward the end of the *Life*, the

---

71. Davis ("Crossed Texts," 14–18) posits that Thecla acted as a critical "intertext" in the later lives of cross-dressing monastic saints; she is explicitly evoked as a model in the *Life of Eugenios*. But see Van Pelt ("Thecla") who argues a more complicated relationship between Thecla and these later hagiographies. On a fulsome reading of these hagiographies as stories of trans men, see Betancourt, *Byzantine Intersectionality*, 89–120.

72. An imperial law from 390 strictly forbade women who had "cut off their hair" (and with "shaved heads") from entering churches or participating in religious rites. As the law was collected in the fifth-century Theodosian Code (16.2.27), it is not impossible that it was known in the general time and place in which the *Life* was composed. Even so, the author either feels that Thecla's unique status as God's virgin, or the failure of her attempts to disguise her gender, shield her from this law. (My thanks to Paula Fredriksen for reminding me of this law's promulgation.)

73. Van Pelt, "Thecla," 222.

author once more makes clear that Thecla dons male clothing precisely in order to disguise her feminine beauty: "without any delay, she left Antioch, putting on again something more manly to wear in order to conceal with her outfit the shining bloom of her youth—for none of these misfortunes was able to bedim or obscure her beauty, which instead was made more honorable and conspicuous by the beauty of her soul" (*Life* 25.3). Just as assaults, executions, and other travails cannot obscure Thecla's womanly beauty, neither, we assume, will "more manly" clothes. "The virgin" who rejected fiancé, marriage, and home is persistently reinscribed as feminine even at those moments she seeks to efface that femininity.

The paradoxical persistence of Thecla's gender status, despite her flamboyant rejection of sexuality and all of its social obligations, is of a piece with the more conservative sexual politics of the *Life*. If the *Acts* could be understood as subverting gender norms and hierarchies (even if, as Andrious and others have argued, modern scholarship may be exaggerating that subversion),[74] the *Life* is much more comfortable with those norms and hierarchies, reiterating over and over the conservative standards of feminine modesty that Thecla breaks only out of extraordinary Christian fervor. Castelli proposes that "the *Life* blunts the ascetic drive that pulses so sharply through the earlier narrative, reframing the promotion of celibacy in terms that do not condemn marriage altogether."[75] Paul's preaching does echo some of the more radical anti-marriage teachings found in the *Acts*: he promotes and praises virginity and celibacy. But alongside the promotion of virginity comfortably sit commendations of married life. While preaching in Onesiphorus's house Paul states: "I affirm that this is also very good and procures the same blessedness [as virginity]: choosing marriage and pitching a wedding tent, just as God commanded it, but having enjoyment of wives only insofar as to give life to others from them and in their stead: surely this differs in no way from virginity in terms of dignity" (*Life* 2.6). In his defense before Cestillius, the judge in Iconium, following a long condemnation of idolatry and polytheism, Paul notes: "Now marriage also is a medicine of God and an aid which has been bestowed upon the common race of humanity" (*Life* 7.11).

---

74. Andrious, *Thecla*; Hylen, *Modest Apostle*.

75. Castelli, *Martyrdom and Memory*, 151. Hylen ("'Domestication' of Saint Thecla"), who does not find radical sexual subversion in the *Acts*, disagrees with such assessments of the *Life*.

Introduction

Even Thecla's own behavior is occasionally, if ambiguously, transformed in the *Life* from radical gender subversion to conservative adherence to gender norms. While in the *Acts* Thecla remains silent during her first martyrdom ordeal because she is still gazing upon Paul (actually, Christ in Paul's form), in the *Life* her silence is due to her virginal modesty: "For nothing is so proper for a woman, nothing so fitting, as silence and keeping quiet" (*Life* 12.1). An even more substantial change comes during Thecla's second martyrdom and her famous "autobaptism." In the *Acts* it is fairly clear that Thecla's intention in diving into a pool of man-eating seals is to acquire the baptism that Paul had earlier denied her (*Acts* 34). In the *Life*, however, the "baptism" that Thecla seeks is in fact the equivalent of baptism acquired through martyrdom, as she prays to God: "'If you see fit, cloak me at last in death: release me from this fear through the baptism of death; release them from their toil against me. If I give up my life then they will give up entirely the violence and tyranny against me'" (*Life* 20.6). Finally, while one of the most iconic moments of Thecla "surrendering" her social gender identity—giving her bracelet and mirror to the jailers to gain access to Paul in Iconium—is retained in the *Life*, it is also subtly undone after Thecla survives her second martyrdom. As in the *Acts*, the governor provides clothing for Thecla, who had been stripped naked for her ordeal; but in the *Life* "he ordered that she be dressed in suitable clothing and that she receive ornament fitting for a reverent and temperate woman" (*Life* 23.1).

None of these incidents straightforwardly restores Thecla to the normal social and sexual status of her gender: while retaining her modest silence during her first martyrdom, Thecla delivers a plea to "Paul" in the stands, expanding a brief instance of speech in the *Acts* (*Life* 12); while reframing the autobaptism of her second martyrdom as "the baptism of death," the author then has no qualms about portraying Thecla catechizing and baptizing members of Tryphaena's household and "many" during her remaining life in Seleucia (*Life* 24.1; 28.1); and the "suitable" ornament and clothing received from the governor in Antioch is soon enough replaced with "something more manly to wear" when she goes off once more to seek Paul (*Life* 25.3). The result of this back-and-forth between gender conservatism and subversion is that only Thecla is allowed to slip, occasionally, out of the frame of social norms. Thecla's rejection of home, marriage, and sex is contextualized within a broader accommodation of sex, marriage, and reproduction. She remains the dazzling exception rather than a role model for future radicalism: the "stranger" whose strangeness allows her to stand outside the routine workings of family life, even as they chug along.

There are a few ways we might understand the author's "blunting" of the *Acts*' ascetic message in the *Life*. He may be reflecting a more developed Christian society in which ascetic life was the vocation of a highly honored but numerically tiny portion of the Christian populace: monks, male and female, were understood to be a religious elite whose extraordinary measures were not direct models for the average Christian but instead glorious exceptions to everyday human mediocrity. Like elite athletes, dedicated virgins showed the great magnitude of human potential without making any specific demands on "normal" Christians beyond piety and admiration. Or perhaps we should understand the more generous attitude toward married Christians in the *Life* as present even in the seemingly more robustly ascetical narrative of the *Acts* as well: as some scholars have argued since the 1990s, the apocryphal acts may have always been more about patriarchal power and control than about feminist subversion or liberation.[76] We should also not lose sight of the agency of the author of the *Life*: it may well be that a man who has dedicated his life to the service of "the virgin" does not see her as a role model of sexual revolution and so has crafted a narrative that emphasizes her uniqueness and "strangeness" rather than her revolutionary appeal.

Miracles Versus Magic

Thecla's "strangeness" is also evident in the miraculous events that occur around her in the *Life*, sometimes invoked by her prayers but just as often bestowed upon her by the invisible hand of God. While the *Life* was written before the *Miracles*, and that second half of the double-work seems to have gone through multiple editions and redactions, it's clear in the writing of the *Life* that the idea of a catalog of the saint's miraculous deeds is key to understanding the saint's *Life* as well. The miracles that happen *to* Thecla in the first part portend the miracles effected *by* Thecla in the second part. The penultimate chapter of the *Life*, in which Thecla settles outside Seleucia, sees her "fortifying" herself against the demons who reside there, a segue into her many demon-fighting, disease-removing, wish-granting deeds to follow in the *Miracles*.[77]

76. Cooper, *Virgin and the Bride*; Andrious, *Thecla*; and Hylen, *Modest Apostle*.
77. In *Life* 27.13–14 Thecla routs the demons Sarpedon and Athena from the

Introduction

The miraculous events that occur to Thecla in the *Life* are all drawn directly from the *Acts*: the rainstorm that extinguishes the fire of her first martyrdom, the protection of the "meanest" lioness in the course of her second martyrdom, the lightning flash that protects her during her self-baptism, and the inability of any of Alexander's machinations to destroy her at all. Thecla's charmed life leads the governor in Antioch to suspect her of sorcery: "He asked who she was and what she had done to appear stronger than the beasts, coming perhaps to an indecent suspicion and idea not suitable for Thecla." The author notes that it is not uncommon for non-Christians to find "the wonders of the saints" to be "suspect": "They don't suppose these are God's or the indications of a pious soul, but the results of some kind or sorcery or magical art, judging what we do according to their consistently evil actions" (*Life* 22.2). This leads to an excursus on the difference between divine miracles and blasphemous magic. Magical acts, the author asserts, are effected through immoral means: "homicide and animal slaughter and other such foul deeds" (22.3). He gives a short list of famous pagan magicians who were no doubt guilty of such "polluted" acts, before turning to praise the simple acts of biblical heroes who accomplished "great things" through God: Elijah, Moses, Peter, Paul, and, of course, Thecla.

The suggestion in this excursus that divine miracles are clearly and unequivocally distinct from pagan magic belies centuries of Christian unease with that very distinction. The confrontations between apostles and "magicians" that the *Life* cites—between Paul and Bar-Jesus in Acts 13:6–12 and between Peter and Simon Magus in the apocryphal *Acts of Peter*—are meant to naturalize the difference between (Christian) magic and (non-Christian) miracle. But, as Shaily Shashikant Patel has argued, such "clear" distinctions are often part of an anxious apologetic discourse designed to separate Christians from non-Christians where otherwise such separation might not be apparent.[78] As Patel further argues, the blurring juxtaposition between Christian miracle and non-Christian magic in these early texts is also strategic: "This new movement is promoted as an alternative to magicians and their wares, but our texts concurrently leverage magicians' appeal to promote their own protagonists and, by extension, emergent Christianity." That is, by bringing "miracle" and "magic" into close proximity in order to distinguish the two, these texts also invite comparison. The sharp rhetorical divide between magic and miracle allows early Christian texts to

---

outcropping by Seleucia; these exorcisms comprise *Miracles* 1–2.

78. Patel, "Notes on Rehabilitating 'Magic.'"

The Life of Thecla

draw on the very real appeal of "magical practices" while staking a claim to be something different (what will be known as "religion").[79]

The *Life* participates in this double-sided discourse: repudiating "magic" (as in this excursus in *Life* 22) while also drawing on the allure of magic throughout the text. The *Life* is redolent with images and language associated with "magical" practices in late antiquity. In the *Acts* we are told that young Thecla "did not move from the window" from which she could hear Paul preaching next door (7–10; trans. Elliott). The *Life* provides a more vivid description: "as she began to apprehend some phrases of the divine address, immediately she was stung in her soul by his words and she was transfixed to the window as if by the steely nails of Paul's speech" (*Life* 1.13). "Steely nails" that sting Thecla's "soul" would conjure the image of binding spells, *defixiones* or *katadesmoi*, common ritual instruments in the ancient world for exerting one's will over another.[80] Typically the spell would be inscribed on a durable surface (like lead), folded over to conceal the words, and then "transfixed" with nails to hold the spell in place (and symbolically "bind" the spell's target).[81] The suggestion here is that Thecla is not just drawn to Paul's words: she is literally enchanted by them. Indeed, when Thamyris discovers Thecla with Paul in the jail he is enraged to find "the girl truly bewitched (καταμαγγανευθείσης, *katamagganeutheisēs*) . . . by Paul" sitting "as if bound to him" (*Life* 10.7).

Similarly, when Alexander first sees Thecla (in the *Life* this happens from a great distance) he is struck as if by a magical spell, "seized by the girl's power" (*Life* 15.7). After she humiliates him by ripping his military cloak and pulling off his crown, Alexander is torn "between opposite temperaments of enchantment (φίλτρου, *philtrou*) and hate" (*Life* 15.17). We might expect here "love (φιλία, *philia*) and hate"; the author instead chooses a word, *philtron*, that is also used of love spells to drive home the fact that Thecla, like Paul, casts apostolic enchantment wherever she goes.[82] During the parade of beasts before Thecla's second martyrdom, when she is "bound to" the meanest lioness, who suddenly becomes docile and protective of Thecla (*Life* 16), the "binding" language recalls

---

79. Patel draws on the sociological work of Wendt, *At the Temple Gates*, on competing "freelance ritual experts" in the first Christian centuries.

80. My thanks to Sarah F. Porter for first pointing out the resonance of this language here.

81. See Gager, *Curse Tablets*; and Nasrallah, "Judgment, Justice, and Destruction."

82. For a similar use of *philtron*, see Porter, "A Church and Its Charms."

the binding spell evoked in the first chapter of the *Life*. Finally, and most explicitly, after Thecla baptizes herself and is protected by a divine flash of fire, the sympathetic women in the crowd "introduced a multitude of perfumes and fragrant oils and vaporized them through the fire and so cast a spell (κατεκήλησαν, *katekēlēsan*) on the beasts with the variety of scents and lulled them into a deep sleep" (*Life* 21.2).

That apostles and saints might be mistaken for magicians and sorcerers is part of the narrative of early Christian literature from early on. The *Life* is thus participating in a long tradition of cagily defining Christian miracle as distinct from magic while blurring the lines between divine intervention and magical "enchantment." We might push the author's fascination with miracle and/as magic further than mere literary trope and recall that, as a devotee and habitué of Thecla's shrine, invested in a decades-long project to catalog her miraculous interventions, he may have seen many pilgrims and supplicants equally ignorant of, or at least uninterested in, the distinction between a love-spell and a saint's divine intercession. While our author might make pious noises about the difference between magic and miracle, what mattered at the end of the day for the author and his audience was one thing: the saint's power.

Trinitarian Theology

Another minor theme that has been added to Thecla's story by the author of the *Life* is explicit attention to creedal orthodoxy. This additional element is to be expected in a fifth-century reworking of a second-century story. At the outset of "the virginal history" the author provides a standard Trinitarian formula affirming the coeternity of the Son and the Father using explicitly Nicene terminology ("there never was a time when [the Son] was not with the Father," *Life* 1.1). Paul's preaching in Iconium that so enchants Thecla is primarily about bodily and spiritual morality; he does, however, reiterate the coeternity of Father and Son briefly in his *apologia* before the Iconian proconsul and even uses the key Nicene term "consubstantial" (ὁμοούσιος, *homoousios*) (*Life* 7.8). Even in that long speech, however, his primary aim is to demonstrate the falsity and immorality of polytheism in arguments that recall second- and third-century Greek apologists. Paul's direct preaching to Thecla in jail, which has no counterpart in the *Acts*, is a moral exhortation to fortitude in the face of the devil's snares and wiles (*Life* 9). It is surprising, then, that when Thecla encounters Paul after her ordeal in Iconium, she praises God in highly Trinitarian and Nicene language, giving thanks to "the divinity in Trinity which is unchanging, of equal power, of equal station" (*Life* 13.6).

When Thecla finds Paul again in Myra after her ordeal in Antioch, she praises the apostle by reciting a litany of "the things I have acquired through you and through your teaching," beginning with the Trinity (*Life* 26.1). Thecla praises the "consubstantial Trinity" six times in a series of ever-expanding propositions about the Trinity's nature, equality, unchangeability, omnipresence, and its paradoxical and ungraspable condition. This orthodox recitation is obviously more expansive than anything we have heard Paul preach (or Thecla learn) to this point. Most of the rest of her list of things learned pertain to the redemptive work of Christ incarnate, the punishments and rewards that await all souls, and the benefits and rewards of chastity and virginity, as well as of "prayer, fasting, and charity" (23.18). Insofar as Paul then praises her in return and announces her suitability for "apostleship and divine preaching" (26.23),[83] readers can rest assured that Thecla's instruction to future disciples will be totally and completely orthodox.[84]

While beefing up Thecla's orthodox *bona fides* for a fifth-century audience, the author also deftly sidesteps debates that were gaining momentum during the period of his composition. Just a decade or so before our author wrote the *Life*, Nestorius, the bishop of Constantinople, had been condemned at a council in Ephesus for (in part) refusing to endorse the total union of human and divine in Christ and the application of the term Theotokos (God-bearer) to the Virgin Mary. The sole reference to the mechanics of the incarnation that were so at issue throughout the fifth century are gently veiled in Thecla's theological oration in *Life* 26: "through you I have come to know the great mystery, which is beyond every rational and intelligible notion, of the birth of the Only-begotten according to flesh" (26.10). Thecla makes no mention of the Virgin Mary, nor does she dwell on human and divine natures or refer to the language

---

83. Another slight shift in Thecla's radical independence in the *Acts*, where Thecla independently announces her intention to go off and preach with Paul's subsequent assent (*Acts Thec.* 41).

84. The author also mentions that, in his day, the wall of Thecla's shrine is decorated with gold *tesserae* "proclaiming to all people the holy and elevated consubstantiality of the Trinity" (*Miracle* 10; trans. Honey). The saint had prevented an Arian bishop of Seleucia from destroying the mosaic (presumably in the late fourth century).

of unions, juxtapositions, or distinctions that roiled the churches of the eastern Roman Empire at this precise period.

It is worth noting that the author's own bishop, Basil of Seleucia, with whom he quarreled so vociferously, was involved in many of the twists and turns of the christological debates in the 440s and 450s. Basil was present at "regional" episcopal meetings in Constantinople in the late 440s where key figures in these debates were elevated or disciplined. He was among the bishops assembled at the Council of Ephesus that deposed the bishop of Constantinople in 449; he was also present at the Council of Chalcedon in 451 that overturned that Council of Ephesus and created a new orthodox Definition of the dual natures of Christ in the incarnation. Given the opacity of Basil's own opinions at these highly charged and political councils,[85] it's perhaps too much to imagine that the conflict with Basil about which the author of the *Life* complains in the *Miracles* (see my discussion above) was grounded in theological disagreement. In an era of high theological tempers, the author's reticence to place definitive christological dogma in Thecla's or Paul's mouths might be more prudence than piety.

Though the author may display theological reticence, he does permit himself high literary flourishes, even in the midst of Thecla's theological recitation. When Thecla notes that she has learned from Paul the terrors that await the damned after death, her language is highly classicizing: "Through you I have come to know that hell (Ταρτάρου, *Tartarou*), the fire, the river of flame (Πυριφλεγέθοντος, *Pyriphlegethontos*), the terrors and punishments and tortures in Death (ἐν ᾅδου, *en Hadou*) are boundless and impartial" (26.15). While it was fairly common by this period for Christians to use the classical term "Hades" for the realm of the dead or as a personification of Death, the other two terms—Tartarus and Pyrophlegethōn—are rare. As distinct regions of the pagan underworld, these terms (along with terms like Styx and Acheron, other underworld rivers) were used by a few earlier Christians in a comparative sense: either to show how pagans (incorrectly) understood the afterlife or to show how some enlightened pagans, like Plato, correctly anticipated the punishments of hell preached by Christians.[86] Their presence here, as part of a theological recitation, is a literary flourish

---

85. As detailed in Wuk ("Pragmatic Necessity"), who also explains the various councils and meetings at which Basil was in attendance.

86. See, for instance, Ps.-Clement, *Hom.* 1.4 and Eusebius of Caesarea, *Praep. ev.* 11.38. Other Christian writers with high rhetorical training sometimes use these terms poetically, like Gregory of Nazianzus and John Chrysostom.

typical of an author who fancied himself a member of the regional *literati* as well as a deeply pious devotee of the saint.

Textual History and Translation

Dagron prepared his critical edition from twelve surviving Greek manuscripts. Of those, only four contain both the *Life and Miracles*:[87]

> Athens, Ethnikē Bibliothēkē tēs Hellados, gr. 2095, fols. 152v–227v (12th cent.)
>
> Moscow, Gosudarstvennyj Istoričeskij Musej, Sinod. gr. 26, fols. 1–64 (11th cent.)
>
> Vatican, Biblioteca Apostolica Vaticana, Vat. gr. 1667, fols. 335–364 (10th cent.)
>
> Vatican, Biblioteca Apostolica Vaticana, Vat. gr. 1853, fols. 94, 96, 5, 38, 45, 39, 44 (10th cent.; palimpsest underwriting fragments)

The remaining eight contain only the *Life*:

> Mount Athos, Monē Philotheou, 9, fols. 219r–235v, 244–261v (11th cent.)
>
> Milan, Biblioteca Ambrosiana, A 63 inf., fols. 86r–148r (13th cent.)
>
> Paris, Bibliothèque de nationale de France, gr. 521, pp. 7–139 (12th cent.)
>
> Paris, Bibliothèque de nationale de France, gr. 1521, fols. 219r–259v (12th/13th cent.)
>
> Paris, Bibliothèque de nationale de France, Supp gr. 240, fols. 7–9, 151–152, 164–175, 177, 179–180 (11th cent.; palimpsest)
>
> Venice, Biblioteca Nazionale Marciana, gr. Z 586, fols. 200–242 (12th cent.)
>
> Vatican, Biblioteca Apostolica Vaticana, Vat. gr. 796, fols. 250–304 (16th cent.)
>
> Vatican, Biblioteca Apostolica Vaticana, Vat. gr. 1643, fols. 131v–161v (11th cent.)

---

87. Dagron, *Vie et miracles*, 140–51.

INTRODUCTION

In addition to these twelve manuscripts, Dagron was aware of two other *Life and Miracles* manuscripts—Berlin, Staatsbibliothek zu Berlin (Preussischer Kulturbesitz), Philipps 1446 (42), fols. 1r–62v (17th cent.) and Vatican, Biblioteca Apostolica Vaticana, Vat. gr. 655, fols. 178v–239r (16th cent.)—which he reports as apographa (direct copies) of Vat. gr. 1667. And another two of the *Life* have yet to be evaluated: Moscow, Gosudarstvennyj Istoričeskij Musej, Sinod. gr. 179, fols. 182–224 (11th cent.) and the fragment in Milan, Biblioteca Ambrosiana, Q 6 sup., fols. 93r–93v (13th cent.; palimpsest). As Dagron notes, most of these manuscripts also contain other Thecla-related hagiography, usually the much more faithful rewriting of the *Acts* by the tenth-century hagiographic compiler Symeon Metaphrastes;[88] one also contains the *Acts*, with its original short ending (Vat. gr. 1853).

As is clear from this quick rundown, the *Life* was of more interest to later readers than the *Miracles*, which were never transmitted separately. This may be due to the uses to which such texts were ultimately put: as lectionary readings on saints' feast days, during which hagiographic *vitae* were typically read in whole or in part. It may also be due to the familiarity of Thecla's life story, ensured by the (much wider) circulation of the *Acts*: readers were more interested in an adaptation of a familiar story than they were in a totally new set of stories featuring Thecla set in the fourth and fifth centuries. The *Miracles* may also have struck later readers as too parochial, focused on the remote shrine of Hagia Thekla rather than the broader eastern Mediterranean terrain of the *Life*. Even on its own, however, the *Life* was never terribly popular: its dozen plus manuscripts are dwarfed in number by the manuscripts of the *Acts* or even of the later version of Symeon Metaphrastes. As a product of its specific time and place, the *Life* did not have apocryphal legs. Precisely as a product of its specific time and place, however, the *Life* gives us insight into a key chapter in the afterlife of a saint whose legacy looms large throughout Christian history.

One curious piece of evidence for later Byzantine reading of the *Life and Miracles* (apart from its sparse manuscript transmission) is a composite text that may date from anywhere between the sixth and ninth centuries entitled (in some manuscripts) "The achievements of the holy apostle and protomartyr Thecla in the Myrsineōn (or in Myrtle Wood)."[89] Dagron

88. Greek text and Latin translation in *PG* 115:821–45.
89. Dagron retains the title "Achievements (Κατορθώματα) of the holy apostle and protomartyr"; other manuscripts have the title "Miracles (θαύματα) of the holy protomartyr" (see Kaestli and Rordof, "La fin de la vie de Thècle," 51).

The Life of Thecla

includes this text as an appendix in his critical edition and Honey translates it in her dissertation along with the *Miracles*.[90] The first part of the text is a cover letter from an unnamed person to unnamed emperors ("most divine rulers") written to accompany "the true image (εἰκόνα, *eikona*) of Thecla." In the second part, the author gives an account of the origins of this sacred icon. It was originally commissioned by a libidinous pagan priest of Seleucia who caught sight of Thecla near her dwelling place in Myrsineōn (although its accurate execution is the result of the miraculous inspiration of the iconographer). The painting was passed down through the pagan priest's descendants to "Achaius, a nobleman [ἰλλούστριον, *illoustrion*], a learned philosopher, and a Christian man."[91] During his life he allowed copies to be made and, after his death, the original was publicly displayed. The third part of the text recounts some miracles of Thecla and an account of the end of her life that is similar to the longer "long ending" found in later versions of the *Acts*. That this is a composite text is clear from its composition and its circulation in various middle Byzantine manuscripts: some contain all three parts, some only the second and third, some only the third.[92]

The connections of this multipart account to the *Life and Miracles of Thecla* are clear: the mention of Achaius connects the shrine in the fifth century to its apostolic origins; the location, Myrsineōn or "Myrtle Wood," is mentioned as a location near Hagia Thekla in *Miracle* 23; and, as I discussed above, the extended ending of Thecla's life disappearing into the rock seems to be a response to and expansion of the *Life*'s version of the end of her life.[93] It is patently subsequent to the *Life and Miracles* and uses its details to craft new stories about the saint. The story of the icon (with or without the cover letter to "the most sacred rulers") also survives, in whole or digest form, in several defenses of icons compiled during the iconoclastic conflicts of the ninth century: all of these texts attribute the letter and the story of the icon to Basil of Seleucia.[94] The use of these few scant details from the *Life*—including, perhaps, its early erroneous ascription to Basil?—to authenticate icon-veneration, recount additional "miracles" of

---

90. Dagron, *Vie et miracles*, 413–21; Honey, "Thekla," 440–46.

91. The technical term from Latin, *illustris*, indicates that Achaius is of senatorial rank; the text also specifies that he was the "administrator (παραμονάριος, *paramonarios*) of the martyrium of Saint Thecla."

92. See Kaestli and Rordorf, "La fin de la vie de Thècle," 50–89.

93. Dagron, *Vie et miracles*, 348.

94. Kaestli and Rordorf, "La fin de la vie de Thècle," 34–36.

Introduction

the saint, and to expand upon her astonishing non-death might, ironically, testify to the obscurity of the *Life and Miracles* by the period in which this composite tract came together. There are no efforts to cite the *Life and Miracles* as an authoritative text on Thecla or her veneration; instead it has dissolved into the undifferentiated sea of hagiographic legend, providing convenient details for future story-making.

Various elements of the *Life*, and the physical copies of the *Life* itself, became embedded in a textual tradition of hagiography and the annual commemoration of saints throughout the Christian year. But the specifics of the literary production of the *Life* in the fifth century should make us question some tidy periodizations of ancient and medieval Christian literature set in the age of Christian origins: *apocrypha* or *martyrologies* or *hagiography*. The *Life of Thecla* shows how robustly so-called apocryphal materials could be repurposed and refashioned into a literary showpiece that at times recalls classical history, evokes formal oratory, and conjures tales of magic and miracle. Like the character of Thecla herself the *Life* is excessive: it exceeds our expectations of genre and highlights the ongoing creativity of Christians celebrating their heroic pasts and imagining triumphant futures.

For my translation I have used the text of Dagron and his chapter divisions, adding my own descriptive titles for each chapter. In marginal notes I signal corresponding passages from the *Acts* as I believe many readers will benefit from the comparison; direct citations from the *Acts* are in italics as well. I also include the few biblical and classical references, mainly allusions rather than direct citations, in marginal notes. Footnotes mainly provide context or clarification for obscure or complex passages. I have also inserted headings for the invented speeches to signal the author's primary literary contribution. As the author's style is (despite his protestations) rather elevated and at times quite dense, I have taken the liberty of breaking up his frequently long sentences with creative grammar and typesetting, while never altering his meaning. I have also attempted to retain at least a flavor of his recherché style.

The Life of Thecla

The Deeds and Miracles of the Holy Apostle and Martyr of Christ, Thecla.^A

Deeds.^B

Preface

¹This text at which we have toiled is a history and an account of the ancient deeds performed by the blessed Thecla, the apostle and martyr. It has been taken out of another, older history and put together following in its footsteps.^C ²Let it be known that we have embarked upon so great a task as this not as though we were saying anything more extensive or more beautiful or even more accurate than what was said before, but as a way of fulfilling our personal vow: to devote something from our meager and lowly abilities to the great martyr who, because of her goodness, takes pleasure in the smallest things. ³We were also eager to bring to completion the command of a pious man,^D of

---

    A. Dagron takes this title from the oldest extant manuscript while removing the erroneous ascription to Basil of Seleucia.

    B. The two parts of the work are, in Greek, "Acts" or "Deeds" (πράξεις, *praxeis*) and "Miracles" (θαύματα, *thaumata*). To avoid confusion with the *Acts of Thecla*, this first part is usually referred to as the *Life of Thecla*.

    C. That is, the *Acts of Thecla*.

    D. Achaius, whom the author names at the end of this preface. He is mentioned again (without his name) in the last chapter, and not at all in the *Miracles*.

whom perhaps I shall make some mention in one way or other in my writing. ⁴Nonetheless I should see fit to note to those who will read this text, in the present and perhaps in future, that if something additional has been said by us—for so it has been—we haven't done anything outside the purview of classical writers.^A ⁵For while we have followed the intent and order of what was said and done at the time of the martyrdom, just through a different (so to speak) style and vocabulary, we have adapted the task previously undertaken by others and dedicated it to the greatest martyr. ⁶By weaving speeches into it where possible, we have imparted to it (at least I think so) an old-fashioned beauty, while keeping the particular and distinct form of speech for each character. ⁷We have concerned ourselves very little with classicizing^B vocabulary or old-fashioned expression, instead we have paid attention to truth and clarity and to order of events, so that nothing at all of what was said or done by the apostle and martyr should be unknown, nor indeed any of the things said or done by others because of her.

⁸Herodotus of Halicarnassus and Thucydides the Athenian,^C and whoever after them was among those who wrote ancient or recent histories, each affirmed that they embarked upon their task of writing due to their own inclination and interest. ⁹But as for me, I embarked upon the history of the apostle and martyr Thecla after being frequently incited by a divine message and urged by the advice of the best of men—I mean Achaius, the best and wisest of all. ¹⁰Not out of fear that these things would become obsolete or obscure as time went on—for the actions of the saints remain forever secure, steadfast, and immortal, preserved by God both for his own eternal fame and for the benefit of the people still dwelling on earth—but so that we might adorn our own selves through this sacred task, so that we might fulfill that vow which we brought forth long ago, and so that we might make clear to future people the man who charged us to do it. ¹¹This is also what the wondrous

A. Literally, "writers of old." On the invention of "classical" authorship in late ancient Christianity, see Chin, *Grammar and Christianity*.

B. Literally, "atticizing," a reference to the formal rhetorical style predominant since the "Second Sophistic" period of the second and third centuries.

C. This invocation of the "fathers" of Greek historiography signal that the author sees his literary project as distinct from biography or hagiography.

Luke has clearly done in both the divine Gospel and in the book concerning the apostles, affixing Theophilus at the beginning, to whom indeed he dedicated the entire task of the divine writing. Now I shall begin here the virginal history.

Luke 1:3; Acts 1:1

Thecla Hears Paul Preaching in Iconium

Acts Thec. 1, 7

1 ¹While the Word of God was born from God and the Father from the beginning and for as long as the Father existed (for there was never a time when he was not the Father, being eternally with the Son and eternally abiding with each other, the Father with the Son, the Son with the Father, light with light, eternally living water with eternally living spring);^A ²and he was also born, and became incarnate, from the holy Virgin Mary, eternally unwed, in recent days and roamed the earth for the salvation of the human race (which is why he became a human), then was the band of apostles established by Christ himself while setting things in order on the earth; but the many and countless flocks of martyrs also sprouted up and rained down after Christ's own ascent into heaven. ³This, in turn, was the time when Thecla lived, not after lots of other men and women martyrs; rather, she was the second one immediately after the apostles and Stephen the martyr (whom the word of truth acknowledged as first), the first among women. ⁴As a result, Stephen leads the way among men fighting on behalf of Christ and because of Christ, while Thecla leads among women, also fighting in similar contests.^B This is what happened.

Acts 7

⁵The divine Paul, who started out as a Jew and a persecutor, zealous for his ancestral law, as he himself says somewhere, but who was found worthy of divine baptism, of preaching, and of being an apostle—how this was we have learned from the blessed Luke—and was finally hewing to his apostolic course. ⁶Now then, as this Paul was racing around the world for the instruction, calling, and salvation of the gentiles he came also to Iconium so that

Acts 22:3–4; Gal 1:13–14; 1 Tim 1:13

A. The author locates Thecla's story in the larger sweep of divine history, like Gospel accounts (particularly echoing the Gospel of John here).

B. While the author does not use the title "protomartyr," which attached to Thecla by the sixth century, the idea is present already here.

The Life of Thecla

cf. Acts 14:1–5

he might preach piety even in that place. ⁷This is a city of Lycaonia, not very far from Oriens, but rather anchored in a part of Asia and lying on the outskirts of the territory of Pisidia and Phrygia. ⁸Having come there, and having been found worthy of Onesiphorus's welcome and hospitably welcomed as his guest, he also became the neighbor of the virgin Thecla.^A ⁹Unintentionally and without pressing for it, he was guided by the Holy Spirit so that, from such close proximity although unseen, Paul might convey the faith to the virgin and emanate and shine down the rays of piety to the girl still sitting under the gloom of error. Indeed, that's what happened. ¹⁰For while he was teaching in Onesiphorus's home, and many were listening, gathered together in the same place because of this, the virgin—who started out as part of a noble family, from among those exceedingly distinguished by nobility, wealth, and beauty; who was already old enough to marry and who frequently incited anxiety and dissension among many of the well-born young men (on account of what always incites anxiety and dissension for well-born young men in love who want to marry the most beautiful and best woman); ¹¹but who was nevertheless, through her mother Theocleia, engaged^B to Thamyris, a man more well-born than the sort of well-born men who were found throughout that city, superior to all others in all things; and whose nuptials were still in a state of delay and postponement—the virgin was by one of the windows in her home which was itself next to another widow that was in another house, that of Onesiphorus, and this is how she heard Paul's voice.^C ¹²At first she was awestruck, as she was hearing a strange and unfamiliar voice (just as Christ wanted, so that such a pretty thing might be ensnared). And as she began to apprehend some

2 Tim 1:16;
4:19

A. The author omits several chapters recounting Paul's arrival to Iconium (including a famous physical description of the apostle), being met by Onesiphorus and his family on the road, and Onesiphorus's unpleasant exchange with Paul's duplicitous companions, Demas and Hermogenes (*Acts Thec.* 2–4).

B. The author uses an unusual verb here, προσομιληθεῖσα (*prosomilētheisa*), which in a general sense may mean "be associated with" and in more specific instances can connote conversation or even sexual contact.

C. I retain this long sentence (beginning with "For while he was teaching . . .") to give a sense of the author's elaborate prose style. In the *Acts*, the reader doesn't meet Thecla until after Paul's preaching.

The Life of Thecla

phrases of the divine instruction, immediately she was stung in her soul by his words and she was transfixed to the window as if by the steely nails of Paul's speech.[A]

Paul's Teaching on Purity

Acts Thec. 5–6

2 [1]What sorts of things was Paul saying?

Paul: Preaching on Purity

[2]"Men, you have gathered together to hear from me, a strange preacher, something strange and incredible;[B] and while I shall truly say strange and incredible things, they are nevertheless divine and salvific; they are things I have learned from the Word of God himself, who was born and appeared on earth in a human form and nature and taught us this angelic and heavenly way of life.

cf. John 1:14

[3]"How blessed[C] is that one who is a genuine contemplator of God, who has kept his soul unalloyed, unmixed, unsullied from these human evils!

[4]"Blessed in turn is that one who does not abandon his flesh to the most shameful of the pleasures, as he will see God without impediment forever!

[5]"That one is no less blessed who, although having been born according to the law of nature, proceeds through life as if he were never born at all, pure and undefiled, and enjoys this life only insofar as he enjoys the best things, which are pleasing to God, but does not enjoy the worst things, which upset God.

[6]"I affirm that this is also very good and procures the same blessedness:[D] choosing marriage and pitching a wedding tent, just

---

A. On the invocation of "magical" language, see the introduction, p. 32.

B. The phrase "strange and incredible" (ξένον καὶ παράδοξον, *xenon kai paradoxon*) appears in some earlier apocryphal texts, such as *Acts John* 88, and is a favorite phrase of the fourth-century preacher John Chrysostom.

C. In the *Acts*, Paul pronounces a series of sayings modeled on the Beatitudes in the Gospels, each beginning: "Blessed is the one who . . ." Here the author creatively uses different forms of the word "blessed" in his series of exhortations, a variation of the Greek rhetorical figure of speech known as polyptoton.

D. The author introduces the "blessedness" of chaste marriage on equal

as indeed God commanded it, but having enjoyment of wives only insofar as to give life to others from them and in their stead: surely this differs in no way from virginity in terms of dignity.

⁷"Then again someone might affirm that they share in equal blessedness who, out of reverence and fear of the divine, take care for the chastity of their souls and bodies, who also take care that their virginity, always the best thing, is intact and who imitate the life of angels while on earth, so that they might share completely in the same freedom from passion and the same portion.

⁸"By much more still indeed I deem those blessed who also keep safe and sound the grace of their baptism, and who do not stain the garment of Christ through shameful deeds or words, but preserve it in the same condition in which they received it from the beginning until the end. ⁹I have also considered those worthy of imitation who are anxious for the sufficiency of the needy and the poor, who seek after the same mercy from the greatest God.

¹⁰"But besides all of these it is necessary always to keep faith in Christ and affection for him undiminished, unshakeable, unwavering, unchanging, and without stumbling. ¹¹While the head of the virtues is always unwavering and unchanging, the whole body of piety will also be healthy, and it will easily head straight to heaven, and there it will share at last in the kingdom and glory and portion, and will have the benefit of those divine and intact crowns and rewards: most blessed is the one who attains these, while the one who misses the mark is the most pitiable, I suppose, and truly worthy of punishments in Death."

Thecla Rejects Her Family

3 ¹So, speaking and advising, divine Paul was revealing such things to those citizens who were always present; as a result he led each member of his audience, be they men or women, into a great and boundless desire for his words of piety; ²and the house was overflowing with a great throng and that street was overflowing with men as well as women, the young and the old as well, all with delight neglecting food or drink and neglecting their work

---

par with virginity, which is not present in the *Acts*.

The Life of Thecla

in their homes and in the marketplace, hanging upon only the speech and the teaching of Paul.

³That virgin stayed in her home and was still clinging to that most beloved window: for the modesty of her age, and the law that those who were still virgins must not gad about but must keep quiet inside, still constrained her noble desire and persuaded her to stay inside; although she felt sick and complained, she had no idea what she might do in the meantime. ⁴Although others were present and listening, she who was not there and had not seen Paul was more gripped by Paul's words; and she was clinging to the window, as though it were administering that most beloved voice to her and rendering her in no way inferior to those who were looking upon Paul and surrounding him.

⁵The girl was so serious and determined that she was by no means willing to step away from the window, to have a share of food or water, or to beautify the neglected parts of her body with clothing, dabs of perfumes, colorful make-up, and braided hair (as is the custom for girls). ⁶This worried Theocleia—whom the tale recognizes as the girl's mother[A]—and led her to a suspicion and an ignoble fear. That she was so excited about the stranger and had abandoned everything that was necessary and pleasant in life engendered the unfair suspicion that came naturally to those with no experience of the matter.[B] ⁷And so, as quickly as she could, her mother sent for Thamyris, as he alone might be able to persuade and redirect the girl who was being guarded for him.

⁸For indeed even, as is often the case, before the sexual embrace and intercourse take place, a certain desire comes to exist for those who have as yet only been joined together by words. The young man desires the girl, of whom he has not yet had any experience, and the young lady desires the boy; ⁹before the wedding feast and the bridal chamber, she converses already with him as if with a husband, although she is not wed to him; and although the wedding lies in the future, a certain pleasure and a gracious delight creep up in their respective thoughts. ¹⁰And

---

A. As in the *Acts*, no father of Thecla is present in the narrative. By "the tale" (ὁ λόγος, *ho logos*) the author may mean the original *Acts*, as he already named Theocleia in chapter 1.

B. That is, Theocleia thinks Thecla has fallen in love with Paul.

before the marriage-bed, as seems natural, they talk about what comes after the marriage-bed. Accordingly Thamyris came when he was summoned. He was dreaming of what he hoped for, and because of this running eagerly, but he found what he had not hoped for, and because of this laid blame on his haste. For immediately Theocleia used words like these with him:

Acts Thec. 9

THEOCLEIA: PLEA TO THAMYRIS

[11]"My humiliation precedes my words, Thamyris, along with my tears; I feel shame before saying anything and I cannot bear the insult against my child at what I am about to say. All the same, though, hear about this calamity from someone who doesn't want to speak of it! [12]For your Thecla has gone far outside our prayers and hopes for her; she spurns me, her mother; she spurns you, her fiancé; she doesn't want to know at all about what's going on in this house. [13]She desires some stranger, a swindler and drifter, who is occupying the house next door—to the detriment of our house!—so that he may take her prisoner and depart, as if out of some mill-house or brothel.[A] [14]So now hurry up and rush to her, Thamyris, and even while she gazes at another man snatch her away from his clutches; summon her back to us and preserve the ancient good fortune of your family and mine. Let us not become a shameful tale, a most wicked story for all humankind. [15]Indeed, use tender and complimentary words on her, and, as if with some oil, soften the unyielding and defiant nature of her soul with flattery.[B] This stubborn and rigid attitude would never be able to yield to force but might instead be relaxed by persuasion and softening words. [16]So then go to her graciously and with compliments, and perhaps you will draw her back to you and

---

A. Dagron (*Vie et miracles*, 183) posits that this phrase is "without doubt a proverbial expression" ("sans doute une expression proverbiale"). But several earlier (Euripides, Lysias, Philo of Alexandria) and contemporary (Socrates Scholasticus, *Codex Theodosianus*) sources refer to mill-houses as notorious sites of imprisonment, enslavement, and prostitution: see Hillner, *Prison*, 171 and McGinn, *Economy of Prostitution*, 28–29 for sources. My thanks to Mark Letteney and Julia Hillner for guidance on mills and ancient incarceration.

B. Later, Paul warns Thecla that the devil will try to use "compliments and flattery" to dissuade her from her devotion to Christ (*Life* 9.11).

return her once more to freedom and order and to the modesty and temperance[A] befitting virgins and girls."

Thamyris Pleads with Thecla   Acts Thec. 10

4 ¹As Theocleia said these things and implored him, immediately Thamyris was filled with a whirling dizziness, and he sank from immeasurable joy to immeasurable grief. Nevertheless, he went in to the virgin, downcast, timid, and tearful, still at a loss as to what he might say to her; while scarcely bearing up his grief he said such things to her:

THAMYRIS: PLEA TO THECLA

²"I am at a loss as to how I might begin my conversation with you, girl most beloved of all to me! For what you've done now has reduced me and your mother to helplessness. What's going on with you now accords neither with your customs and manners nor with your previous modesty and dignity. ³It is an assault, I think, from some twisted and evil demon who is trying to turn you out of your right mind, overturn the previous good fortune of your household, and attach to all of us shameful reproach instead of most noble acclaim. ⁴Nonetheless be persuaded now by me, your Thamyris: for I am yours, even if not yet in marriage, then already by law and by the agreements I've made with you. Now turn away from that window, turn away from lending your ear to that stranger and vagrant who—I don't know how!—has snuck in to do harm throughout this city. ⁵Let no untoward story about you make the rounds, like:[B] 'The child of noble Theocleia, fiancée of Thamyris, first of the city, but now spurning all of it: wealth and family and mother and the noble tales of her family, even

---

A. "Temperance" (σωφροσύνη, *sōphrosunē*) and cognate words are used throughout the *Life* to describe both the conventional modesty of well-bred people (as here) and the rigorously virtuous celibacy prescribed by Paul and embraced by Thecla. On the ascetic shift in this term in the fourth and fifth centuries, see Clark, *Reading Renunciation*, 113–15.

B. The well-educated Thamyris includes his own invented speech within the invented speech by the author.

more her previous upbringing and education; she has been stolen away by some stranger and vagrant, the pride of the city has become the plaything of some sort of prisoner or supplicant. ⁶He serenades while sitting by one window; she has been ensnared by his songs while clinging to another window. And her mother is ignored although she exhorts her and sticks by her at all hours; she ignores her fiancé—in a short time her husband!—as he admonishes her and begs her. She belongs entirely to *that one* and to his words and deceitful spells!' ⁷Now then hurry, most beloved, and flee from such accusations and reproaches; stop your listening to that polluted voice, put your modesty and temperance before this tricky and strange pleasure; finally, leave behind that window: it's no place for a well-born girl and will be no help at all to your good reputation! ⁸If my speech doesn't strike you as vulgar, since you are still a virgin, let us consummate this longed-for marriage, with the propitious divinity!"ᴬ

⁹Thamyris used these words and yet still more of the same sort while Theocleia was pleading together with him: badgering her daughter to be convinced, proffering her breast and gray hair, begging not to be dishonored by this irrational sickness. ¹⁰But the virgin was entirely unreceptive to these words: she was fixed firmly to Paul's voice alone, refusing so much as to look at Thamyris or give heed to her mother as she exhorted her. ¹¹She was like those women who have been seized by God, seeing only one thing: that to which the longing and speech on Christ's behalf drew her. Because of this the house was filled with wailing and lamentation and everything became full of dejection and grief.

Acts Thec. 11, 13

Thamyris Meets Paul's False Friends

5 ¹This was the state of their home when Thamyris got up and ran off from the house; he came to Onesiphorus's outer door, pressing on to Paul himself. But he stopped his rush when he happened upon Demas and Hermogenes there. ²The two of them were not good men but were pretending to be. They were with

---

A. In an attempt to persuade Thecla to abandon Paul, Thamyris suggests they consummate their marriage sexually.

Paul; now what they were did not pass by unnoticed,^A but were to that point enjoying the apostle's goodwill, either so that they might be improved from such an association or so that in the end they might have only themselves to blame for the ill-advised way they persisted in evil. ³For that very reason Thamyris was asking them who this stranger was, and from where—talking about Paul—and what he wanted and what he was saying and doing. ⁴Demas and his companion made note of the man's haste and anger—for it did not escape them that Thamyris was full to bursting with anger—and they immediately laid bare the poison long hidden and smoldering in their entrails, since now it had an opportunity to act against Paul. They said to Thamyris:

DEMAS AND HERMOGENES: ACCUSATIONS AGAINST PAUL

Acts Thec. 12, 14

⁵"Most noble of men (which is already clear to us from what we have seen and what we have learned of you, for most things can be determined as virtuous or evil by sight and sound), about these things you ask us now, listen as truth leads the way! ⁶As for this stranger: where he comes from and who he is we don't exactly know because he is a cheat and a drifter, a reject from the common social order and from correct social structure and he has corrupted all things—this we know, and indeed most clearly, from what we have often been taught by that one. ⁷For he is even trying, with all his might, to cast out, overturn, and corrupt the path of marriage and procreation contrived by nature herself for the human race. Through certain new and bizarre teachings he is eager to confound all human nature together, legislating *celibacy* and theorizing^B about *virginity*, new terms now and for the first time expressed by him. ⁸And he is trying to proclaim and introduce some sort of resurrection of bodies long dead and dissolving into the earth, a new subject not yet heard from anybody, even though the true and accurate 'resurrection' is preserved and

---

A. That is, Paul is not fooled by their dissimulation of friendship and loyalty. In the *Acts*, it's not clear if Paul believes their loyalty but Onesiphorus is suspicious of them upon their meeting.

B. Literally, "philosophizing."

The Life of Thecla

accomplished every day in human nature itself: for the succession of children begotten from us is this and wants this, with the image of those sowing and reproducing being renewed again forever in their children, and so in a certain way again 'resurrecting,' such that we seem to see those who long ago passed away in the living people who are once more with us."

Acts Thec. 13, 15–16

Paul is Arrested

6 ¹After Hermogenes and Demas said these things, Thamyris was brimming with even more anger; but as if he had acquired the most surefire public declaration against Paul, at present he grew calm and he turned his attention to a banquet; he no doubt received those men as guests and invited them in as if making a deposit of this banquet for the price of their malicious accusation against Paul, so that he might render them even more enthusiastic later.ᴬ ²Right when the day began, not so much as waiting for the sun to rise, with some partisans and advocates,ᴮ and with people accustomed to daring anything, he set upon Paul. Each of those accompanying him had anger as a weapon and the tool of each one's craft could be found in their hands. As this went on someone eventually cried out:

"SOMEONE": DENUNCIATION OF PAUL

³"Let him be hit! Let him be bashed! Let him be dragged to court, this cheat and offender, this inventor of new laws alien to nature, roaming about for the destruction and corruption of the cities,

---

A. The *Life* moves the banquet after Demas's and Hermogenes' slander against Paul (in *Acts Thec.* 13 it comes first), making it a bribe for future testimony rather than an incentive to provide information. The author also removes the suggestion from Demas and Hermogenes that Thamyris bring Paul before the governor (in *Acts Thec.* 14), rendering it Thamyris's own initiative.

B. In *Acts* 15 Thamyris descends on Paul with "leaders and officers" (ἀρχόντων καὶ δημοσίων, *archontōn kai dēmosiōn*); the author of the *Life* replaces these officious sounding companions with similar-sounding words for rowdy sports fans (δημοτῶν, *dēmotōn*) and legal experts hawking their skills in the *agora* (ἀγοραίων, *agoraiōn*).

who acts wickedly and abominates marriage, which was devised for temperance and the creation of legitimate children, and who instead, on the pretense of virginity, legislates fornication!"

⁴As he was still saying these things many others also came forth, insolent and rash men, insolently and violently leading Paul. Everything was full of shouting and disturbance and howling, as if some soldiers were suddenly attacking a town and pillaging everything. ⁵Thamyris ran toward the courthouse with them in great strides (as someone might say poetically); he was leading Paul with his own hand to the court as if he were casting some tyrant from the Acropolis.^A Entering through the courthouse gates and standing at the tribunal he began with these words: cf. Homer, *Il.* 7.213

THAMYRIS: DENUNCIATION OF PAUL

Acts Thec. 16

⁶"I suppose, Judge, that this is a sign of the gods' favor and of your own good fortune: that this destroyer and polluter, residing here to do evil to the entire city, has been brought out into the open and under our laws. At last let it be for you and your judgment to render assistance to the empire presently established, and to render assistance to the laws, to be of aid to the common condition of humanity which is in danger of no longer existing. ⁷How this is I shall say in brief: This man standing here before your bench and your court, who he is in sum, or where he has come from, I cannot say: for this person is a stranger, unknown to all of us. ⁸Inside this unassuming form and figure, as you can now see, he is producing some new and bizarre teaching against the common race of humanity, blaming marriage, which is—as someone might say—the foundation, root, and source of our nature. ⁹Look what has come to light from it: Fathers, mothers, children, families, cities, districts, and villages; sailing and farming and all sorts of trades of the earth; empire and commonwealth and laws and reigns and law-courts and armies and commands; philosophy and oratory and the entire stream of speech; and, what's greater, shrines and sacred precincts and sacrifices and rituals and initiations and prayers and litanies! ¹⁰All

cf. *Acts Thec.* 3

A. The author juxtaposes a Homeric allusion with an erudite (if somewhat inapposite) reference to the casting out of the Tyrants in ancient Athens.

of these things, and as many more that we have left aside because of a surfeit of words, are accomplished and done through people, and the person is the product of marriage.

¹¹"This man, of whom I was speaking, blames marriage and reproaches it, and he persuades all to hate it; he praises instead a kind of virginity, which I can't even define at this point, but I have heard some saying that he praises and marvels at celibacy, at not having intercourse or living together according to the law, neither husbands with wives nor wives with husbands, but embracing childlessness and solitude. ¹²This is nothing else than condemning everything all at once to destruction: families and nations and cities and villages and districts and professions and works and occupations and simply everything, and, to put it succinctly, leaving the earth desolate and uninhabited. For if all people were convinced of this, this human race would quickly fail to produce life. Now I have told you what has been said and dared by him in summation. ¹³But now let it be for you, Judge, to demand punishment for him, as one arrested for the greatest evils, and render assistance to all of us whose greatest and first prayer is to take a wife, to kindle the wedding torch, to sing the bridal song, and to leave behind children, and the children of children; render assistance to that most excellent marriage, from which you yourself came and by which you acquired children. Undoubtedly you will look upon many and marvelous grandchildren, befitting to you as their grandfather and great-grandfather, if you do not delay in your judgment!"

¹⁴Once these things had been said by Thamyris, Demas—or perhaps it was Hermogenes?—standing a little ways off, quietly and quickly suggested:

DEMAS OR HERMOGENES: ACCUSATIONS OF CHRISTIANITY

"Correctly, cleverly, and wisely have you spoken out against this Paul! But you have neglected to add to your statements the one greatest point: that he is a Christian. This is especially adverse to the laws,^A and this will place him more quickly under punishment and will lead to the pit of his destruction."

Paul's Apologia Acts Thec. 17

7 ¹When Thamyris had made his statement, the judge next asked Paul who he was and from where and what he had been doing: "For you are not at all unaware of what has been said against you by Thamyris," he said. Now then Paul said:

PAUL: DEFENSE AND DENUNCIATION OF PAGANISM

²"Proconsul, most noble of men, I am neither the creator nor the inventor of my teaching, for which they now accuse me. Its true creator, teacher, and legislator is God, who took mercy and pity on this human race and who has sent many others and now me as a herald of his compassion for all of us. ³As a result he is cutting away and drawing out the illness deeply rooted in us, which from the beginning overwhelmed us out of ignorance, error, and deceit; we can make public, disclose, and show to all people the evils of idolatry concealed long ago, I mean the rituals and initiations, the animal sacrifices and murders, which have made inroads into this life through myths and certain appealing stories, filling up the earth with every impiety and loathsomeness. These have by no means been spoken of nor tallied up but are altogether unspeakable and accursed.

⁴"For it is especially through these things, these myths or fabrications, that the real God has gone unrecognized, the one who is both steward and creator of the universe, while some tens of thousands of demons were worshiped:^B demons of fields, of hell, and agitators; promiscuous demons, malevolent and avenging and ill-omened and pitiless, forever desiring lawless murders,

---

A. Like the *Acts*, the *Life* imagines an anachronistic legal "ban" on Christianity already in the time of the apostles.

B. Paul's defense here recalls Christian apologies of the second and third centuries, which defended Christian monotheism by attacking the immortality of pagan polytheism.

The Life of Thecla

forever thirsting for their share of meat, for slaughter and smoke and gore and burning fat and blood, in return for earthquakes, in return for famines, feeding on and afflicting everything under the sun! ⁵But what's even more unholy and abominable than these things: for indeed through these most excellent myths, adulteries, fornications, pederasties, incests, and corruption of children were venerated and honored. Isn't it because of these that we get Aphrodite and Ares, Hera and Zeus, Zeus (again!) and Ganymede, the swan and Leda, and the bull swimming through the sea with Io?^A ⁶About dogs and sheep and cows and—still even worse!—cats and hawks and crocodiles made into gods, what more could one say? How did the expounders of your polytheism not blush when they made these things into gods, and transfer them from earth into heaven?

cf. Rom 1:20–28

⁷"I myself have been frequently amazed, and I am still amazed! Because of these and all the other wicked sorts of impiety, God is the one (as I said) who has mercy and pity on this nature, as the one who formed and created it and so has allotted us, the apostles, through his only-begotten Son, to go out and visit the entire world and purify it from those evils of which I spoke and those I omitted. ⁸We are to introduce instead faith, knowledge of God, piety, which above all are designated and certified by the Father, Son, and Holy Spirit, the holy and venerable Trinity, the uncreated and consubstantial divinity,^B eternal and immutable, indivisible and limitless, beyond time and the universe, of the same honor and throne and glory, ungraspable, incomprehensible, on which all things have depended and to which all things extend, and there is nothing which has been separated from it. ⁹After this we are to proclaim also that the Word of God dwelled among humankind with flesh: for while he is from God and is God and is always with the Father, he appeared also with flesh, born according to the common law of human nature, but from a virgin and unmarried woman, so that he might rescue his formation and creation and free us from the ever tyrannical

---

A. Either the author or Paul is confusing his myths, as Zeus transformed into a bull swam through the sea with Europa (he changed Io into a cow to hide her from Hera).

B. Paul uses language crafted in fourth-century Trinitarian theology, such as the term "consubstantial" (ὁμοούσιος, *homoousios*).

demons ¹⁰and, even beyond all these things, so that he might teach us holiness and temperance, and advise us about chastity and virginity and holy abstinence, and advise those who are willing and convinced to set out on the path to God through virtue and perseverance, but not so that he might require those who are unwilling or unconvinced to yield to these divine laws and decrees—for neither force nor fear could ever become the creator of virtue. Noble things are voluntary and not compulsory.

¹¹"Now marriage also is a medicine of God and an aid which has been bestowed upon the common race of humanity and is also an antidote to fornication and a kind of source and channel and succession of the common race, devised by the creator of all himself for salvation, protection, and longer life of human, as people succeed one after the other and renew the ever perishable nature over and over, until the time for the consummation and the resurrection makes to pass away this form of the world and brings to pass instead a better and more divine portion.^A ¹²For the mortal must be clothed with immortality and the corruptible changed into incorruptibility, and all of us must run back once more to our former homeland and city, which place is heaven, whose builder and creator is God. cf. 1 Cor 7:9

1 Cor 15:53

Heb 11:10

¹³"I proclaim these things, I teach these things, because of them I wander the whole earth, because of them even now I have come here: whoever wants to and is able, let him judge me for these things and let him persecute me! For I am prepared to rush headlong into every trial and danger on behalf of truth."

Thecla Visits Paul in Jail   Acts Thec. 18

8 ¹When Paul responded in this way to Thamyris (inciting no small amount of wonder at what he said clearly and frankly on behalf of the faith) the proconsul found no cause for punishment against Paul from the great hue and cry of Thamyris or from his diatribe and rabble-rousing speech; then again he found some of the apostle's speech praiseworthy but other parts laughable, as if   cf. Acts 23:29

A. As in his preaching in Onesiphorus's house, Paul makes clear that he endorses marriage and reproduction, a concession notably absent from the *Acts* but more in line with fifth-century Christian morality.

The Life of Thecla

he were listening to strange and novel stories. ²At that time, he contrived to create some postponement in the uproar and the matter against Paul: he ordered him thrown into prison so he might hear from him again.

³After these things happened in this way, and as that great disturbance and tempest were dying down, the virgin had no idea what had been done and so was experiencing great anxiety over what would happen next to her teacher. ⁴But when she was informed of everything by the rumor racing all around, she contrived and executed a plan too impetuous for a girl, too masculine for a woman, and too fervent for a fully initiated Christian. ⁵She removed her adornment—for she had a lot, and it was worth a lot—bracelets, earrings, necklaces, and all the rest of the vulgar inventions of women, and with them she bought her way to see and look upon Paul. For her desire for piety was leading her into more daring plans and actions. ⁶She bribed a certain enslaved member of the household, one posted at watch at the gates; she paid him with her bracelets and so rendered the rogue more compassionate and in this made him a traitor to the woman who owned him.^A ⁷She encountered him and left the house, her heart pounding, trembling and changing color at an undertaking so daring and uncharacteristic of a girl; nevertheless she went out and, faster than you could say it, she made her way to the prison, at once taking advantage of an opportune moment for such stealth: for the night was deep and dark, providing plenty of safety for both fugitives and thieves.^B ⁸Then with similar bribes she also cajoled the jailkeeper—for he was a local soldier,^C very easily induced by greed, and a betrayer, of the

---

A. In the *Acts* both the gatekeeper and jailer bribed by Thecla are at the jail. In the *Life*, which often endorses highly archaic and conservative ideas about gender segregation, Thecla must bribe her way out of her own house and then take a dramatic and fearful journey through the darkened city.

B. The lover seeking her beloved through dark city streets evokes Song 3:1–3.

C. Literally "a city soldier" (στρατιώτης ἀστικός, *stratiōtēs astikos*), a military officer posted inside the city. The fourth-century orator Themistius refers to the commonly known "greed (φιλοκέρδεια, *philokerdeia*) of the city soldier" (*Or.* 8.114).

sort for whom betrayal is frequently a danger to their soul—and finding the gates free to her she ran in to Paul.

⁹Coming in and just appearing nearby she astounded all those who were then present and inspired great awe, such that they were all made faint; and she astounded Paul himself, since she dared something more audacious than is typical for a woman or a girl, but she did not make him entirely give up on the hope in Christ.^A ¹⁰Therefore he addressed her and sat her down next to him; he shared divine and heavenly words which it was necessary to share, and through which it was possible for her to be betrothed and escorted down the aisle to Christ, explaining—I imagine^B—this sort of thing:

cf. 2 Cor 11:2

Paul's Teaching to Thecla

PAUL: EXHORTATION TO THECLA

9 ¹"As you see, my girl, I have been bound up because of you, having been indicted by your fiancé Thamyris. I was in pain until the present, not because I was bound up or locked away—for at no point have I forgotten what I have already suffered, and what I shall suffer, and what I am determined to suffer on Christ's behalf—but because I was afraid, indeed exceedingly afraid, that having been bound I would never make any use of these bonds and I would leave this city without fruit or profit, restoring no one to life and leading no one to Christ.^C ²But look! You have appeared to me, coming from who knows where, and you have relieved this fear! From what I have suffered because of you, and perhaps what I shall suffer, already I see my harvest begin to grow. I consider you my harvest, you who have just now run to me, you who intimate that my crop of piety and faith is already fulsome and mature. ³For this very first thing—being kindled from that

---

A. That is, despite her immodest behavior Paul still hopes to convert her.

B. Here is one of the moments the author explicitly signals his use of invented speeches, perhaps in this case because the *Acts* do not report any of Paul's teachings to Thecla in prison, so this instance of speech is completely the author's invention.

C. Presumably the throngs of men and women of all ages crowded around Onesiphorus's house to hear Paul dispersed at his arrest.

small and faint spark of my words; then immediately spurning mother, wealth, family, a city of no small significance, and a fiancé of great distinction; then, having already lifted up the cross, being prepared to run the course of the good news—how much joy do you suppose has filled the heaven, the powers in heaven, Christ himself? ⁴As for him I think right now he is smirking down at the devil who, once upon a time, gloated and grumbled against all human nature but who now will be made sport of and quickly demolished by you alone, still a tender young girl!

⁵"Just let no fear upset you, my daughter, let no trick deceive you, let no earthly longing divert you, let no fire or iron put off this noble confession. Do not have a female and unmanly disposition; do not, now that you have surrendered yourself to the King of Heaven, still be anxious about the Tyrant, even if from the highest reaches he casts temptation before you, even if from somewhere in the clouds he wages war against you, even if he mobilizes every instrument of impiety against you, every arrow and snare. ⁶He will use many and countless things to delude you: through words, through actions, through promises, through whippings, through flattery and compliments, through fire and even through beasts, through judges and the public and executioners.ᴬ ⁷If he should sense just a little your persistence and power in Christ, he will quickly scurry and scamper off faster than you could say it; he will flee from you more than from that Job whom at one time he besieged with myriads of evils, but whom he then proclaimed his conqueror.

⁸"But come now: I shall describe for you in speech the Enemy, my daughter, you whom I bring forth in these bonds of mine, so that you might be able to discern him well and easily. ⁹As for this one who seems fearsome to humans: on the one hand he is audacious, shameless, daring, thoroughly depraved, quarrelsome, and belligerent; but he is also unpredictable, cunning, full of compliments, crafty in every trickery and clever in his machinations, transforming and changing himself before all those people who always fall before him. What's more he is cowardly, flaccid, ignoble, and weak, knowing only how to run away from even the slightest serious threat. ¹⁰If he sees some Christian who is fearful,

---

A. Thecla will indeed face all of these, except whippings.

The Life of Thecla

cowardly, careless, loving life more than God, he sets upon him, he faces off with him, he mobilizes every machination against him—through pleasures and through sufferings—until he has separated that pitiable and wretched one from the noble hope and faith, and he draws him down into his abyss, suitable just for him. ¹¹On the other hand, if he sees someone steadfast and virile, of exalted disposition and mind, fortified with the weapons of faith, such a one he approaches from the start through compliments and flattery and this sort of artifice, gently and quietly serenading and enchanting him, and attempting to entice him and drag him down with the appetites of this life, so that by taxing his endurance he might strip away his piety. ¹²If he should catch sight of someone who has in no way given up, who has not yet given in, who has not in any way been captured by such things, but who is steadfastly and firmly resisting, then he will finally come at him through more fearsome weapons, terrifying and frightening him, baring a sword, lighting a fire, goading judges, rousing publics, arming executioners, and preparing beasts. ¹³If he sees someone standing up to these things, the faithful soldier of Christ standing ready until death and slaughter, immediately he is undone, he yields and goes numb, he falls down and runs away, he lifts up both of his hands and admits his defeat.^A For the martyr, both when living and in dying, is no less fearsome to him!

2 Tim 2:3

¹⁴"That's what he's like and how he is prepared, my daughter, the one whom you yourself are going to struggle against. But, just as I said, since you have Christ as your king and ally (as he is already your bridegroom) and you have fixed your resolve, succeed and prevail and hold sway! ¹⁵For you will hold sway, I know well, against every scheme cooked up against you, and through it all you will triumph over the Tyrant. Not only through yourself but through many others. For you will make disciples out of many others and you will lead them to your bridegroom, like Peter, like John, like each of us apostles, among whom also you will certainly be numbered, I know this well!"

A. A gladiator in combat could signal his surrender by raising up his hand.

The Life of Thecla

Paul and Thecla on Trial

Acts Thec. 19

10 ¹Likely these and other such things were said in the prison, as one was teaching and the other was being taught. But once more Thamyris appeared to Paul with an even greater and more violent compulsion. For the fact that it had not been up to that moment apparent or evident where Thecla was, fueled more ardent hostility from Thamyris against Paul. ²When day broke and the rays of light began to shine down, all those girls who were enslaved to Thecla and kept watch over the girl were lingering around her bedroom, as if their mistress was about to get up at any moment and make her usual demands of them, demands of the sort a mistress typically made and those enslaved in service provided. ³By the time sun was high over the earth, still no cry had been heard from Thecla, who was usually giving orders to those girls; the enslaved girls said to themselves and to each other, "What is this? Is our young ward still sleeping until now? Has some sort of distress come upon her? Has illness or sudden death fallen upon her, and that's why her voice has not yet come forth?"

⁴As they were still saying these things, and all of them were coming into her bedroom—for the time of day finally gave them reason to suspect something unfortunate—they didn't find the virgin there at all; instantly they filled the house with a cry and wailing, such that Theocleia, upon learning why the cry and lamentation were occurring, became breathless and speechless; ⁵then the whole city was filled with tumult, and the public with distress and disturbance, while others ran around elsewhere trying to find the girl. For they were calling the girl's flight a common misfortune of the city.

⁶Now while this was going on Thecla was sitting at Paul's feet and enjoying the divine teachings with an untroubled and serene mind. That's when Thamyris appeared, as soon as a certain one of the enslaved household members informed him that the virgin was with Paul. ⁷Rushing in and realizing that this was so, Thamyris became even more inflamed and was driven close to madness that the girl was truly bewitched and stolen away by Paul. That she had run away, that she was sitting like this, close up, at the apostle's feet, that she seemed as if bound to him, made certain and unambiguous then to those seeing them the

incorrect and untrue suspicious of licentiousness. ⁸Many have often been impugned not only by a tawdry action but even by an appearance or a rather curious glance. So now this conveyed an equivalent suspicion to those who saw them. It was for those who didn't know Paul and Thecla to suspect something strange and immoral against them, not knowing why the girl was sitting by him or why Paul was speaking with her. ⁹But when Thamyris observed what he would not even expect in a bad dream—Thecla together with Paul!—he started to shake and was agitated all over, such that it nearly ended in his passing out and dying from his excessive anguish. When a passionate rage and jealousy take hold, the misfortune winds up in plain old madness and insanity. ¹⁰Nonetheless, seizing Paul with the partisans and enslaved people he had with him, he led him forcefully to the court, leaving nothing unsaid or undone against Paul from what his anger wanted and his jealousy commanded. ¹¹So it was that Cestillius (for that was the name of the proconsul),^A for fear for Paul (for he had also succumbed to the man, and a certain longing had also entered him for the things he had said about piety) and for reverence of Thamyris and those shouting about that man and what had been done to them so shamelessly and daringly—that a dignified and well-bred girl had been kidnapped and convinced to disregard all the best things and choose the most shameful and dishonored of all things—Cestillius, after whipping him a little, expelled Paul from the city, and he did not suffer anything after more violent than that.

Thecla's Trial Acts Thec. 20

11 ¹Then Thecla was brought before Cestillius, as her mother Theocleia cried out that she should be led forth and administered punishment for her disorderly and bizarre behavior. When she came into view she filled everyone with wonder and amazement. ²Merely being seen she dazzled everyone with her beauty (and

---

A. In most manuscripts of the *Acts* the proconsul's name is spelled Castelius but at least one manuscript (Vat. gr. 797) calls him Cestillius, the spelling preferred in the manuscripts of the *Life*. Both are rather uncommon Latin names, although Cestillius is slightly more common: see *TLL* 2:240, 353–54.

this was a body which had until then been neglected) and she filled the judge with pity and tears and all those public onlookers with admiration and awe at the way her mien and gaze were held high, proud and severe. ³For she was not conceding at all in these circumstances, nor was she shrinking away from them, but she appeared like some young lioness in the midst of many gazelles. The proconsul employed words like these to her:

CESTILLIUS: EXHORTATION TO THECLA

⁴"I see, my girl, that you are not wanting in nobility, gravity, thoughtfulness, and bodily attractiveness; indeed you possess all the finest qualities, which I myself and all those here can surmise from what we see. ⁵I cannot say, then, what you ultimately want when you flee from marriage, a thing which is serious and precious and praised by all alike, both humans and gods. For this law, to speak concisely, fills the whole world with people and other living creatures, and it fills the air with birds, it grants to the sea to nourish what is in the sea. ⁶Marriage is that which corrects the condition of death, introducing those who are to come in place of those who have been pillaged by it, so that our human race is practically immortal, with people always cropping up who replenish the nature, order, and capacity of those who have passed away. ⁷It is the teacher of temperance, and the most excellent limit and guardian, forever inhibiting unnatural pleasures and intercourse through lawful intercourse. It also distinguishes the legitimate from the bastards and those not well born; it is the most accurate guide to good breeding. ⁸It knows how to keep unadulterated the established names of families. It apportions the succession of property to those who are suitable as is suitable. ⁹So why do you run away from marriage, such a sacrosanct and most excellent possession? For your father, who chose marriage and honored marriage, acquired you, who are so beautiful, and marriage has brought forth into light and the present life each of us who is well born. And each of us certainly goes forth from this life but introduces through marriage another of the same sort.

¹⁰"Now as for Thamyris: he is wonderful and well-bred and not unworthy of your bridal bed and marriage. For he is

The Life of Thecla

also distinguished by his family, and by bountiful wealth, and is the most powerful man in the city. You see how he has grown mad for you, considering you his everything, and has attached his hopes to you alone. ¹¹Do not begrudge yourself or him this fortunate marriage; do not begrudge the city the offspring that will soon come from you both, by whom the city will be adorned, and your family will be adorned! You will never leave behind life without a memorial, as children always pass on to children your sort of reputation.

¹²"Now if you have heard something from this stranger and old man, disregard his words and drivel as nonsense and myths, or else you will blame your thoughtlessness on them. For you don't have the age or understanding yet to judge teachings like this, but it is for you rather to be seated with your loom and spindle, which nature has, as they say, allotted only to women. ¹³But listen to me, pass over from this empty deception and foolishness, choose better and more advantageous things, be joined to Thamyris, and become for all of us a cause for celebration and joy and splendor. ¹⁴I myself shall officiate at your wedding, I shall encircle you and I shall encircle your bridegroom with the longed-for crown, I shall pray for this: that I may also celebrate the wedding of your children."

Thecla's First Martyrdom

Acts Thec. 21–22

12 ¹But while the proconsul in this way mildly and gently urged the girl to change her mind, Thecla uttered no sound at all, having determined that it was not befitting feminine decency or virginal modesty to make her voice public at all nor to expose her virginal tongue to a vulgar audience.[A] For nothing is so proper for a woman, nothing so fitting, as silence and keeping quiet. ²She did not share her voice at all with anyone but she stood there—if it is not audacious to say—like a she-lamb, silent before the one shearing her, striving not to utter anything, dreaming about what she might soon suffer because of Christ; by her untroubled stance, without a tremor, she already indicated her perseverance

cf. Isa 53:7; Acts 8:32

A. Thecla's modest reticence to speak contrasts with her "proud" gaze upon first appearing before the proconsul.

in the face of tortures. ³As a great stillness came over them—Thecla giving no reply, Cestillius at a loss as to what he might do, and the public wondering at the girl's firmness and refusal to yield—Theocleia from somewhere furiously cried out:

THEOCLEIA: DENUNCIATION OF THECLA

⁴"Judge! Why do you delay? Why do you put off pronouncing punishment for this *lawless one who is no bride*"—for I shall use her very words^A—"and why do you defer and delay lighting the fire for her? Let her be burned and destroyed, she who spurns glorious and ancestral marriage, choosing instead a life of a courtesan and a woman shamefully enslaved! ⁵She has run away from a bridegroom with so great a bride-price to attach herself to this vagabond and stranger; she has inflicted the greatest shame on her entire homeland, on her family and city, and on me, who gave birth to a child for such evil, so that my life might become a tragedy!"

⁶Deeply suffering at Theocleia's piteous statements, while also keeping an eye on Thamyris (someone with great power who was justly enraged since he was deprived in this way of a most beautiful wife), and furthermore anxious about the teachings pertaining to the Christians that were being bandied about, the proconsul ordered Thecla to be handed over to the fire; this happened so that, at the same time, the power of Christ would be shown plainly and the grace of the martyr would dazzle forth at last, and the trouble Paul took would not be fruitless. ⁷Accordingly, once everyone had collected wood from all over, and when the flame had been raised into the upper air, she was ordered to go up into the blazing fire. As the girl started to do this she looked at the fire and was eager, with great joy and a gladdened soul along with a direct, cheerful, and unwavering gaze; ⁸then Christ showed himself to her in the form of Paul: cheering on her eagerness, encouraging her endurance, fine-tuning her constitution, so that when the virgin saw him (for she truly thought that it was Paul and not Christ) she smiled a little and said to herself:

A. The words in italics come from Theocleia's parallel outburst in *Acts Thec.* 20.

The Life of Thecla

THECLA: PLEA TO PAUL

⁹"See, Paul is looking out for me and guarding me, so that, in case I become discouraged and faint-hearted, and I flinch before the fire, I won't give up the noble and blessed confession. But by Christ, who was preached to me by you yourself, Paul, I shall not betray piety nor shall I dishonor your teaching! ¹⁰Just stand by a little, my teacher, and call down Christ upon me so that he might cool and dampen this fire by the breath of the Spirit and prop up the weakness of my nature with his help!"

¹¹And after these words, having first made the sign of the cross in herself, or rather making her whole self a copy of the sign of the cross by stretching out both of her hands,^A she leapt immediately into the fire and braved the flame boldly and without hesitation, as if it were no different than high noon or a sweltering time of day. ¹²But due to this the flame, forgetting its nature, in reverence and fear of the cross, became a private room for the virgin instead of a furnace, and it did not allow the onlookers to see Thecla naked. Raised up and bent all around, it formed a wall on all sides against their prurient gaze, fulfilling the function of a little bedroom instead of that of a fire. ¹³For so they say that the Hebrew youths in Babylon the Great of the Medes—there were three of them—once encountered that sort of benevolent fire when God tempered that fire.^B ¹⁴But in that case that's all that happened, and the wonder stopped; but in this case even the earth bore witness to the unlawful violence, echoing with some great booming sound, and the sky produced a rainstorm, without first becoming covered in vapors or clouds, which are believed and said to be the indications of rainstorms; it was directed by God to do this for the honor and assistance of the martyr. ¹⁵This water, rushing down from there with huge and numerous hailstones,

Dan 3:21–27

A. In *Acts Thec.* 22 Thecla makes "the sign of the cross," presumably a small gesture; here she stretches her hands out and becomes herself a staurogram. The image of Thecla with hands outstretched was a common way of depicting her (as *orans*, or praying) on pilgrimage flasks and in artwork in late antiquity.

B. Thecla is repeatedly compared to Daniel and the three youths of Daniel 3 (see below, ch. 19); it is quite possible that the original author of the *Acts* intended such comparison by subjecting Thecla first to fire and then to lions.

drowned many of the Iconians, exacting punishment for their audacity in the very midst of that audacity; meanwhile it freed the virgin from what appeared to be fire.

Thecla Is Reunited with Paul

Acts Thec. 23–24

13 ¹While these things were going on in the city, and everyone was cowering in terror and fear, regretting and keenly lamenting the things they had dared against Thecla, Paul was passing time somewhere outside the town in a certain tomb together with Onesiphorus. ²But he wasn't excluded from those struggles and terrifying events but was exceedingly fearful. He went without food and lay prone on the ground, weeping and crying out to Christ on behalf of the girl as she struggled. None of what was happening escaped his notice, since he was near the city, and not a few people had been chattering about these things. ³As the fasting extended, Onesiphorus's children were finally feeling badly under the deprivation and long hunger—for they had nothing for nourishment, no bread, nothing to drink, nothing to cook, as they were fugitives and in hiding—and they begged Paul to let them make their way to town to buy things they needed. ⁴It was only natural that they were suffering: no distress and discouragement touch young children like hunger and thirst, for this is the greatest calamity for children. So they were allowed by Paul to go and buy things; and they left, taking his tunic (there was nothing else for them to do, since they had no money). ⁵At that moment, the martyr who was delivered from the fire, still anxious because of Paul and roaming around, met up with Onesiphorus's children, who, when they recognized her, led her to Paul. She found him hurled to the ground, imploring and asking God for what he already had right by his feet. Then right away the martyr cried out and said:

THECLA: PRAISE OF GOD

⁶"Blessed are you God, King, Creator of the universe, and Father of your great and only-begotten Son; I myself thank you, miraculously freed from the threat of fire and violence, having beheld

The Life of Thecla

this savior and teacher of mine, Paul, from whom I received the good news of the might of your kingdom, the greatness of your authority, the unchanging nature, equal power, and equal station of the divinity in Trinity, the mystery of the incarnation of your only-begotten Son, the boundless activity and power of the Holy Spirit, the unalloyed, genuine, and salvific profit of the faith, the path of true knowledge of God, the present advantage of a manner of life entirely according to God and the blessed reward to come not long afterward."[A]

[7]When Paul heard this he sprang up from the ground, lifted up all at once by the virginal voice as if by some machine.[B] Being somewhere between pleasure and distress, at that point he also began to pray:

PAUL: PRAISE OF GOD

[8]"It is difficult and quite a challenge to find a hymn of thanks worthy of your benevolence, my Master! What speech could befit your goodness, your kindness, power, and wisdom with which you put have put everything together and rule over it—no speech could befit it!—with which you arrange things, apportioning to all of creation as a whole, and to each one of us, your own care and forethought! [9]I thank you nevertheless, as much as a person can, for the salvation—strange and beyond hope!—of Thecla who is enslaved to you: both that your gift has arisen more swiftly than my request and that the tribulation of my perils and pains on her behalf have not been unprofitable. [10]Look! Through my tribulations and bonds and scourgings here a martyr and disciple has been added to your ranks and, soon after, a preacher of the good news! Since it is pleasing to you, this crop of virginity has sprouted forth, which I know well will bear fruit for us in many myriads of virgins! For the seed of this grain is prolific and authentic and worthy of your storehouse."

cf. John 12:24; Matt 13:30

A. This brief recitation of what Thecla has learned from Paul is vastly expanded when she meets up with him again in Myra in ch. 26.

B. A typically florid and convoluted elaboration from the author of the *Life*; *Acts Thec.* 24 merely has Paul "rising up."

The Life of Thecla

Acts Thec.
25–26

Thecla Requests Baptism

14 ¹When Paul had said such things, they all turned from great despondency to joy: Paul himself, Onesiphorus, the virgin, Onesiphorus's children, as they got hold of both drink and food and no one was lacking at all from the things leading to spiritual rejoicing. While they were still eating what circumstance and necessity allowed—there were some greens and bread, and water to drink—Thecla said to Paul:

THECLA AND PAUL: IN DIALOGUE

²"I have been saved through you, Paul, and I have come to the conduct and faith in Christ; but I think it is still not safe for me to be separated from you and to live in this city. For you have learned well how impious and arrogant it is, not just by hearsay but by actual experience. ³So I shall follow you, after cutting off most of this girlish and misleading hair, so we'll readily be able to avoid onlookers who meddle in such matters. This altered form, I think, will overshadow what you call my beauty and attractiveness."

⁴Paul said: "I want to, but I am afraid of both the present time and even more so of you. The former because it is not lacking in debauchery, and you because you have so much beauty and youth, such that it would be impossible for those looking at you to remain calm, no matter how much they want to. ⁵Let's have no other war waged against us, perhaps even more violent than the preceding one, which would rattle your mindset and prepare it to backslide, having grown somehow numb and betrayed by this feminine condition and weakness. This war is difficult enough for men to overcome, even more so for women and for girls who have just come forth from nurseries and private quarters."

⁶Thecla said in return: "But I shall suffer none of these things, for God, who assisted me at the fire will certainly also assist me in the face of other dangers, even if the enemy should devise machinations more convoluted than these against us. ⁷Only you yourself, my teacher, give me the seal in Christ: for having been armed with this weapon I shall cower before nothing, I shall fear nothing, I

shall appear superior to every danger, I shall appear as beyond every trial and demon. Only give me the seal in Christ!"

⁸He said: "Well then, since these things have seemed fitting to you so they shall be: as for now you will join me on this journey and, once you've waited for a little time, you will receive grace through the holy baptism, which is the only undefeatable power of salvation, security, and faith for those who have placed their hope and confidence entirely in Christ."

⁹When he said these things immediately he undertook the journey, after invigorating Onesiphorus together with his children and sending him back to his own city and home.^A But these are the things which were done in Iconium and they had such a result: wonders took place which are beyond human nature but are not unreasonable for divine power.

Confrontation with Alexander in Antioch

Acts Thec. 27

15 ¹Now they were nearing Antioch—I mean Syrian Antioch, the noble and mighty, which can claim to be where Christians were first called by that noble and blessed name; not the Pisidian one, next to Lycaonia, even if the Pisidians should wish it!^B—and they were approaching the gates; what had worried Paul from the beginning befell him. ²While they were not yet entirely visible to all those passing their time at the gates of the city, Thecla's beauty ran ahead of them like some bolt of lightning, lighting upon the eyes of Alexander; it inflamed him completely and set him on fire. ³As a result, the man could not hold off or put off even for a little while that wickedness; but like mad dogs or people possessed by

cf. Acts 11:26

A. As in the *Acts*, it's unclear why Onesiphorus and his family accompany Paul out of Iconium in the first place, or whether they are still living there when Thecla returns to their home after her adventures in Antioch (see ch. 27).

B. This comment suggests that there were conflicting claims over Thecla's legacy among the different cities called Antioch in the fifth century. Given the overall path of Paul and Thecla in the story—from Iconium to Antioch to Myra to Iconium to Seleucia—Pisidian Antioch, located in the central plains of Anatolia, might actually make more geographic sense. As Dagron (*Vie et miracles*, 44) points out, this itinerary would conform to Paul's travels in Acts 13–14. But proximity to Seleucia and prominence make Syrian Antioch a more suitable location for the author of the *Life*.

demons he charged straightaway at the virginal and all-holy body. The passion of lovers begins, so they say, from the eyes, but once the wickedness sinks down into the very soul it renders frenzied and frantic what was to that point temperate.

⁴Now then this Alexander was Syrian by birth, well-born and wealthy, and at that time he was the head of fair Antioch, and he supplied her with every pleasure and delight. Indeed upon this depended the greatest power over the city. ⁵For by nature every populace is a shifty and unstable thing, and they mete out good fortune to those who delight them and drive them mad with pleasure rather than extolling those men who supply what is useful and helpful; as a result, for the most part they exult in those who feverishly excite them[A] with all manner of debauchery and delight. ⁶The people of Antioch are more inclined to luxurious living, and whoever provides them with the makings of pleasures and spectacles and delights is truly a lover of the city, of the public, and of honor. ⁷So this was Alexander, who was in every way splendid and distinguished: as he looked, as he gazed upon the virgin with eyes that were neither pure nor temperate, he was seized by the girl's power. ⁸He went up to Paul as if to a pimp or procurer; although he was in a disordered state he made use of a kind of feigned orderliness: he solicited a lot, he offered a lot, like a man about to burst into flame. But in the end he missed his mark, since Paul denied that the woman belonged to him in any way whatsoever—if indeed it were possible to know for sure that she was a woman! ⁹Then he quite violently made a go at Thecla, entwining himself with her and feverishly pushing against her, so that the virgin cried out and said:

THECLA: DENUNCIATION OF ALEXANDER

¹⁰"What violence! What lawlessness! What thoughtless tyranny! What shameless and brazen debauchery! Having fled to this city as a harbor and a haven of temperance, I am beset in her by the more ferocious waves of depravity! ¹¹For I am a stranger and unknown, but not without a city or reputation or honor. For my city is the

---

A. Literally, "who create a Bacchic frenzy in them," another classicizing touch.

splendid Iconium and my family is distinguished and not a little wealthy! ¹²I spurned marriage and a bridegroom, the illustrious Thamyris for a passion for temperance, for virginity, and for becoming enslaved to Christ in a most blessed enslavement better than any freedom; because of this I was exiled and cast out of the city. ¹³I am not outcast, as *you* suppose, because of shameful passions which are fitting for you, as though I were trafficking in my beauty and offering it for sale to whoever wants it. By no means! ¹⁴May I not bring shame in this way upon my patron, God, and may I not forget in this way what I promised to God, such that I make lies out of the covenants I formed with him through Paul. *Do not force the stranger, do not force the one enslaved to God!*"

¹⁵I could not use more moving words than these phrases of the martyr.[A] As she was crying out in this way and pleading with him not to do anything worse, Alexander increased his violent assault; so the virgin dared and resolved to something more audacious than is typical of a woman: she ripped at his military cloak, that preening and conspicuous garment, she removed his splendid, golden, radiant crown, and she made him a laughing-stock in front of everyone. ¹⁶(On that site a worthy sanctuary was built for the virgin which preserves its structure until today; it celebrates and attests to this victory.[B] Everyone who passes through and looks upon the site together with the shrine immediately calls to mind what happened there back then and seems once more to look upon Thecla triumphant and Alexander stripped, defeated, and derided. I suppose the glory of that site will carry on for all time.)

¹⁷Now Alexander, insulted and disappointed, was subject to opposite temperaments of enchantment and hate; he didn't know what he ought to do, divided as he was between anger and desire, inclining one moment to one and the next to the other. In the end he hurried to the court and handed over Thecla, not

---

A. As the author makes explicit, the last line of Thecla's speech (in italics) is taken directly from *Acts Thec.* 26.

B. The author knows of a shrine to Thecla near the city gates (thus requiring him to place the confrontation with Alexander there, though the location is vaguer in the *Acts*). Dagron (*Vie et miracles*, 233 n.7) posits this may be the site dedicated to Stephen and Thecla (the first martyrs) that Severus of Antioch mentions in *Hom.* 97 (Brière, *Homiliae Cathedrales*, 581).

so much overcome by his anger as giving up on his debauched deed. ¹⁸Truly he might have overlooked and disregarded it, even if the insult had been much more hurtful than this, if only after the insults he had been able to enjoy the passion which had so wickedly come over him. But now the more ferocious cruelty and wildness of the girl made him into her enemy, since he was insulted and despised, and he had completely failed to attain what he unlawfully desired.

Acts Thec. 28

Thecla Entrusted to Tryphaena

16 ¹Although handed over for judgment, the virgin was nonetheless pleased; she was already calling the punishment a victory and a reinforcement of the struggles of the martyrs.^A But since she was mistrustful of Alexander, fearful that once she was left alone and by herself he might take away her virginity by force—the virginity for which all this risk was being taken—she asked a favor of the judge: not that she would avoid any of the preordained tortures, but only that she remain chaste and be kept pure from the defilement of fornication. ²For as unconcerned as she was with cowardice when it came to the dangers, so much was she concerned with the safety of her virginity.

³Now God gave some forethought to this. From among the women who were around her—for rumor concerning this Thecla had brought many women together—he put forward and urged for this a certain Tryphaena (as she was called), in the ineffable way of which he was fond, to always offer to those in such a state means and solutions out of unmanageable and intractable situations. ⁴Now this Tryphaena, distinguished by her kinship with the emperor, abounding in wealth, and cultivating virtue in her way of life and conduct,^B was entrusted with and received Thecla. ⁵She did this as she felt sorry for the virgin, at what she had tyrannically and violently suffered as she incurred

---

A. The *Life* omits Thecla's confession (in indirect speech) in the *Acts* and the outrage of "the women of the city" and instead highlights Thecla's longing for martyrdom.

B. The *Life* adds "virtue" to Tryphaena's description and more sympathy with Thecla's plight.

punishment for her temperance; but she also wanted to have her as a consolation in place of her daughter who had just died.^A The name of the child was Falconilla.

⁶When one day had passed, Thecla was brought forward by Alexander, for she was condemned to punishment through the beasts. Now Tryphaena followed along, not bearing that the one who had just been entrusted to her should already be surrendered to whomever wanted it.^B ⁷Something happened there, a miraculous act truly worthy of a sign from God: the meanest lioness (or so they figured) was bound to Thecla but ignored her own nature, as if she were an enslaved servant who had from the start been reared with the girl; ⁸she sat down beside her and cuddled around her feet, and took special care with her teeth, I suppose, so that nowhere, even accidentally, would she injure or bother the martyr's gospel-spreading feet. This astounded the whole city at once and it filled all the onlookers with a certain speechlessness. ⁹The community of women could not bear quietly to restrain their wonder—although their gender is inclined by pleasure but disquieted by fear—but they were crying out at those acting so daringly against the martyr, not insofar as she was a martyr, but as a woman suffering pitiable things and having to pay an unreasonable penalty for her temperance, for her reverence, and for not surrendering to fornication and bodily licentiousness.

cf. Isa 52:7; Rom 10:15

Thecla Intercedes for Falconilla

Acts Thec. 29

17 ¹When this parade of beasts broke off, as did the outcry from the women, once again Tryphaena took Thecla and brought her back with her, no longer just because of mercy and pity, but thanks now to this one miracle and thanks to what she had seen in a vision during the night. For when evening had fallen, and Tryphaena had gone to sleep, Falconilla appeared to her and seemed to say such things to her mother:

A. The *Life* adds the poignant detail that Falconilla has died "recently" (ἄρτι, *arti*).

B. *Acts Thec.* 28 specifies that Thecla bore an inscribed charge, "sacrilegious" (ἱερόσυλος, *hierosulos*); the *Life* omits this detail, preferring to leave the impression that her crime is refusing Alexander's sexual advances.

The Life of Thecla

FALCONILLA: PLEA TO TRYPHAENA

²"Mother, I urge you to leave behind this great grief on my account; do not weep pointlessly and do not wear away your very soul with lamentations. You won't do me any good through these things and you'll destroy yourself along with me. ³So beg of Thecla, who is living with you, who has become a child for you in my place, that she intercede for me before God, so that I might encounter his benevolence and gentle countenance, and that I might be transferred to the country of the righteous. ⁴For already even here," she said, "there is great wonder at Thecla, at how splendidly and courageously she is fighting on Christ's behalf."

⁵When Falconilla seemed to have said these things and immediately flew away—for this is the nature of a dream: to appear inscrutably, to be visible and converse vaguely and ambiguously, and to fly away again invisibly—Tryphaena got up at these words, being at once pleased and tearful: the bit of suffering from the sight of her daughter and the pleasure at the recollection of Thecla. She said to the virgin, not far off and sleeping right next to her:

TRYPHAENA: PLEA TO THECLA

⁶"My child, God-given child, since God brought you here and cast you into these embraces of mine, so that you might completely alleviate this misfortune of mine, and so you might claim for Christ the soul of my daughter, Falconilla, and so that you might furnish her through your intercession with what was lacking from faith: pray and beg Christ the King to grant to you from his grace the repose and everlasting life of my daughter. For Falconilla herself also begs this of you through the vision which has come to me tonight."

⁷When Tryphaena had said these things, the virgin, who possessed a soul always ready for prayer and who was always beseeching the divine for what seemed right, considering both the suitable form of the prayer and the prayer itself, set to it quickly and without delay. Raising her holy and entirely chaste hands to heaven, this is how she spoke to God:

THE LIFE OF THECLA

THECLA: PLEA TO CHRIST

⁸"Christ, King of Heaven, Son of the Great and Highest Father, who gave me the grace to believe and to be saved, who shined upon me with the light of your truth, who has already deemed me worthy to suffer on your behalf, grant also to Tryphaena, enslaved to you, that her wish for her daughter be fulfilled. ⁹Her wish is for that one's soul to be counted among the souls of those who have already come to believe in you, and to enjoy dwelling and delight in paradise. Extend this reward to her also on my behalf, Christ my Master. ¹⁰For behold, as you see, she has become the guardian of my virginity, she has supported me after your Paul, she has warded off for me the furious passion of Alexander, she is cooling me off in her own bosom after the fright of the beasts. ¹¹For although she is a queen she has humbled herself for me because of longing for and fear of you. On behalf of all of these things she asks for this, she desires this: that her only and beloved child meet with some repose."

¹²As she was praying these and other such things, Tryphaena, crying out something mournful, dirge-like, and piercing, was no longer mourning for her daughter's death but now grieving for Thecla, as she was a short time later going to be caught by the beasts, with a lovely body and so great a mind.

Thecla's Second Martyrdom

Acts Thec. 30–31

18 ¹While Tryphaena was in this state, Alexander came to collect Thecla and bring her to the animal spectacle. Everything had been prepared for it and already the spectators had occupied the arena: they were rowdy and complaining about the delay in time. He said: *"The governor is seated and the crowd is rowdy: give her over, I'm leading off the beast-fighter."*ᴬ ²As a result Tryphaena, stung and inflamed by these words, cried out bitterly and mournfully and Alexander turned tail in flight. Such were the words of Tryphaena:

A. The author does not remark upon it, but this line of Alexander's is another direct citation of *Acts*.

The Life of Thecla

TRYPHAENA: LAMENT OVER THECLA

³"Woe, woe to me, this second and more difficult grief! How these tortures seize me, one after another, and I have no way to get help or consolation from any quarter! For I am childless and bereft of kin, and I am unlucky in widowhood and have been reduced to helplessness on all fronts. ⁴But I seem to have found a way out of these impasses and this surfeit of trouble: I must take refuge in the God and helper of Thecla. ⁵So now, God of Thecla, who told me the good news of your might and pointed out to me the true and straight path of the piety of your commandments, reveal yourself now to Thecla, who is enslaved to you, and help her as she faces dangers, and show all of us that facing danger because of you and for you is truly good and certain. For if she should meet now with some relief, there is no one who will not make a dash for your kingdom!"

⁶While Tryphaena was still saying these things, some city soldiers came, dispatched from the governor with orders that the girl be taken away by force. ⁷Now then Tryphaena was unable to resist and so yielded to the force; she did not simply hand the girl over to them but, grabbing on to her hand, she left with the soldiers, filling the marketplace with her tears and lamentations, beating her breast and wailing over Thecla as if over a corpse, and calling out such things as this:

TRYPHAENA: LAMENT OVER THECLA (*continued*)

⁸"O wickedness of the demons! How greedily they have used these misfortunes against me! I was the unlucky mother of a single child and then, look! I undertake the funeral procession of a second daughter, as you see. And it's harder: I conducted Falconilla to the tombs when she had died, as is the rule, but Thecla is still living and has committed no fault worthy of death. ⁹But so that she not hand herself over to corruption and profane fornication, and defile her soul along with her body, here I am handing her over to the mouths of the beasts. O violence! O tyranny! O city of the Antiochenes, which will be bloated with so much pollution and guilt!"

¹⁰At these words Thecla, having been pierced and in great pain in her soul, let loose many streams of tears; emitting a loud, sharp cry she herself used words like these toward God:

THECLA: PRAYER TO GOD

¹¹"My God and my help: having trusted greatly and placed all my trust in you I left behind my homeland and spurned my mother and despised marriage: now look and see what is being done against me! ¹²Deliver me from these fearsome and untamed beasts, just as you have already set me free so recently from all-devouring fire; give recompense to Tryphaena, enslaved to you, for all her pains on my behalf. ¹³For you see how, in order to please you and keep me a virgin, she withstands every drunken outrage and insult. Because of her and her compassion for me I have not been deprived of my virginity and I have prevailed in Alexander's fury against me. ¹⁴I take up this fight along with the temperance of which you and I are fond, caring little for the beasts, because of you, who are assisting me from heaven and because of her, who is guarding me on earth. ¹⁵This is part of your forethought over me, to provide a harbor among such fierce and untamed waves, bringing me through this great tempest of those beasts."

Thecla Faces the Beasts   Acts Thec. 32–33

19 ¹She stopped praying and a great fear loomed from all around: from the beasts, from those goading the beasts with lashing of whips and noise, from the public's agitation and the confusion of their cries, from the lamentation and wailing of the women. ²For they were also there in a part of the arena and their opinion on the virgin was divided. Some of them rejoiced in what was being done against Thecla, insofar as they were debased and debauched; but as for the others who were temperate and respectable, they grieved over what was happening, and felt pity for the city at this misfortune, as soon after it would suffer some widespread evil at so great an evil act of bloodthirstiness.[A] ³Many of these women even possessed an eagerness and an intention to perish with Thecla, so acutely were they suffering at this terrible and unreasonable misfortune. ⁴While all of them were held in suspense, gawking at this one thing, this strange spectacle, the virgin was brought in, snatched away from Tryphaena's hands, stripped naked of clothing, so that this might be some provocation for the lions to rush against her: for the brightness of bodies always draws the attention of the beasts' eyes.[B]

⁵Once this preparation was made, the mean lioness was once more sent against her, such that the arena was filled with mourning and tears because of it. ⁶To be sure this most excellent lioness was displaying the fury and haste of a lioness, but then as she approached, she appeared instead like an enslaved servant girl: not only did she not touch that holy and all-chaste body, but having laid before those virginal feet she provided her security from the other beasts. ⁷She annihilated the more rash of the she-bears coming at her and destroyed it at once; but as she went out to meet with a lion who was more ferociously darting out against her, she tangled with him and they perished together. This filled the spectators with great distress, since the lioness who was her ally was taken away from her.

⁸But they were entirely unable to understand that the deed that occurred was a sign from God and not from the beast's natural condition.[C] While what had happened before was wondrous, that the lioness would not attack Thecla, it is even more wondrous that she defended her. ⁹For beasts are always beasts and they have the nature they have. It is ultimately for God to alter them into what he wants, and to restrain their assaults and render some of them docile and obedient to the saints but others

---

A. The *Life* once more omits the direct speech of "the women" in favor of a description of their attitudes.

B. Criminals were routinely executed nude by Roman officials in order to humiliate them (see comparative discussion in Berkowitz, *Execution*, 169–73). Perhaps the author's novel alternative explanation for Thecla's nudity is meant to mitigate her humiliation.

C. The author pauses in his narrative account to highlight the miraculous nature of Thecla's martyrdom, anticipating his fuller excursus on magic and miracle in ch. 22.

untamed and vicious to those who are different. ¹⁰Something similar occurred with the fire in Iconium and, if you please, also with the three youths in Babylon. For that fire was truly fire: very hot, all-consuming, destructive—for that is the nature of fire—but, commanded by God, it provided both to them and to her the function of dew and a refreshing breeze. ¹¹As for Daniel, the Hebrew youth whom they say, having been at that time caged up with lions, was released safe and sound from those beasts, it was not because the nature of the beasts desired it but because the power of God made it happen. ¹²But among the Babylonians, among whom this wonder occurred, this is all that happened, that the young man was not destroyed; but here the beasts chose to wage war against each other on behalf of Thecla: how much more outstanding is this miracle among us!

Dan 3:17–27

Dan 6:17–24

Thecla Baptizes Herself

Acts Thec. 34

20 ¹Although this first ordeal was rebuffed, right away a throng of many even more ferocious beasts charged at Thecla. But that martyr's mind was not occupied with fear of the beasts and with their growling: she was entirely focused on her prayer. I think that, as she prayed in interior silence, she used words like these:^A

THECLA: PRAYER TO CHRIST

²"My master Christ, how great is my gratitude to you for your counsel and purpose for me that, although I was a girl, still cloistered and unknown to many, kept for marriage to Thamyris, you led me forth through your own Paul, and you then found me worthy of your seal and grace through him; ³you gave me a taste of labors and dangers on your behalf, in Iconium through the fire and here through these many untamed beasts; you have displayed me in public in the arena, not losing sight of my salvation but exercising my faith in you and my purpose. ⁴For all of this, not yet worthily, I thank you all the same that I have been found by you

---

A. The author again signals that, lacking any direct speech of Thecla's prayer in the *Acts* account, the following speech is entirely his own invention.

The Life of Thecla

wholly worthy of these sufferings and brandings.[A] ⁵Since I see the Enemy, still great and oppressive, always adding more and more to my dangers, I have been afraid, since I am weak by nature and worn down by these evil acts, that I shall grow sluggish in the face in what remains of the struggle and perhaps stay uninitiated and without my crown and—what's more difficult—that I shall slip away from your kingdom. ⁶If you see fit, cloak me at last in death: release me from this fear by baptism through death;[B] release them from their toil against me. If I give up my life then they will give up entirely the violence and tyranny against me."

⁷When she was saying these things (as seems likely), she turned by chance and saw a pool and water and seals swimming in it, beasts who were themselves sea-going and man-eating, and which had likewise been prepared for Thecla's punishment. ⁸Calling out a few brief words to Christ, and so saying: "In your name, Lord, *I am baptized on my last day!*"[C] she leapt into this water, desiring at last the consummation of death and release to Christ. ⁹When this was accomplished, the whole public resounded and rebuked this strange and fatal audacity: to plunge headlong and recklessly into the water that so clearly held death from the seals. ¹⁰While this is what the virgin welcomed gladly, only so that she might meet with the consummation in Christ, the whole populace keened at this—too foolhardy and horrible!—and showered the animal spectacle with tears like snow. ¹¹But the martyr was not overlooked: for suddenly a heavenly fire flashed up and fell upon the waters; it removed from the beasts their ability to act and it cloaked Thecla, who was naked, and provided for her the necessity of a private chamber.

cf. Gal 6:17

cf. Rom 6:3–4

A. The term for brandings, στιγμάτα (*stigmata*), connotes the marks imposed on convicts or enslaved servants, a striking term for high-born Thecla to use of herself.

B. Whereas in the *Acts*, Thecla goes into the "pit" in order to baptize herself, here Thecla more modestly aims for a "baptism through death," assuming she will not survive what is in the pool of water.

C. The same words with a slightly different connotation are spoken by Thecla in the *Acts*.

The Life of Thecla

Tryphaena Swoons

Acts Thec. 35–36

21 ¹But even as these signs from God were happening, no reverent fear came upon the irreverent Alexander. To this throng of beasts he added another throng, like some violent wind rousing up waves upon waves; he didn't realize he was striving to conquer the one who can't be fought against—for who would ever know how to conquer God?—and was already vanquished. ²Now the women spectators, moved by great compassion or even by God, contrived such a thing as this in opposition: they introduced a multitude of perfumes and fragrant oils and vaporized them through the fire and so cast a spell on the beasts with the variety of scents and lulled them into a deep sleep. The result was that, although Thecla was amidst many beasts, she was entirely free from fear among them. ³God has not ever typically struck from his superiority or his power against those acting with unrestrained impiety, but with fleas and frogs and mice and locusts and other such things he has always contended against those who aspire to great power; instead of a serious task he makes a game out of the destruction of atheists who think they're high and mighty, just as was happening here. ⁴As this was happening, Alexander was even more shameless. He said to the governor: "I have bulls, dangerous and exceedingly frenzied; if you just order her bound up to them, we shall quickly see the end of her punishment." ⁵When the governor heard this, he reluctantly gave the order, showing on his face his sorrow at this matter. As for Alexander, he devised the use of fire alongside the natural ferocity of the bulls and was adding it through burning stakes to the underbelly of the bulls. ⁶He didn't notice that he was already vanquished: for the fire annihilated the bulls and burned through the bonds and released the virgin from her bonds, not touching her at all. This clever scheme ended up as its opposite for the clever schemer and deviser against the wisdom and power of God.

cf. Exod 7–10

⁷Even as this threat came to its end, Tryphaena, losing heart at this long duration, swooned and passed out at the magnitude of her distress over Thecla; right away she was brought down from the arena to the Planks—there was a place there called "planks."ᴬ

A. The author supplies an unhelpful gloss to an unusual term from the

The Life of Thecla

⁸This filled the whole city at once with great fear and terror—for immediately the evil event was broadcast—and filled the judge with intense dread. Alexander was shocked and trembling, falling prone on the ground, using such words as these to the governor:

ALEXANDER: EXHORTATION TO THE GOVERNOR

⁹"Mightiest of rulers, I was the one who was insulted and my own body was mistreated by this woman, or demon, or evil spirit—I don't know what I shall call this alien and strange beast, who appears more shameless than all the other beasts! ¹⁰She hasn't suffered from them any of the harm she was supposed to suffer; perhaps out of some witchcraft or some other stronger art and rite she has prevailed in this way over their wild and untamed nature. ¹¹Let her leave here, let her be cast out of the city, let her be taken away to others, let her then be gone at last and grant to others the experience of her strange and more novel nature. ¹²Wondrous ruler, this abnormal fear has shaken and rattled this city all around: for Tryphaena has probably died because of this woman condemned to fight the beasts. If she has truly died, and this becomes clear to her kinsman the emperor, I am the one who shall be destroyed, and the city itself will be destroyed, and you will be in danger, since you overlooked so difficult a tragedy as this. ¹³So if you are convinced by me, cast her out of the city, let us attend to the safety of this imperial woman, if we have any reason or consideration for our own safety!"

Acts Thec. 37

Excursus on Miracles and Magic

22 ¹The governor, quite disturbed at these words but also pleased that he was relieved from such a lawless and violent judgment, called for Thecla to be brought closer. He asked who she was and what she had done to appear stronger than the beasts, coming perhaps to an indecent suspicion and idea not suitable

---

Acts: ἄβακες (*abakes*) usually means tablet or board (and becomes the Latin *abacus*), but in the *Acts* and *Life* it probably means something like gangway or plank.

The Life of Thecla

for Thecla. ²For to those who happen to be ignorant of the divine and of the might bestowed upon holy people from God, even the wonders of the saints are suspect. They don't suppose these things are God's or the indications of a pious soul, but the results of some kind or sorcery or magical art, judging what we do according to their consistently evil actions. But that's not how it is.

³For a person performing magic who wants to create something new and perform some miracle first launches into homicide and animal slaughter and other such foul deeds: for he would not produce any of his strange or unusual things were it not from the abomination and cooperation of these things. ⁴If someone is familiar with Apollonius of Tyana, in Cappadocia, from those who have recounted his life—so we might speak of the most famous of a great many such figures—they are entirely familiar with the polluted and impious implements crafted according to the man's magical craft: ⁵certain invocations of gods and of souls, summoning demons, undetected acts of wickedness, such that he was not eagerly welcomed among the Gymnosophists in Ethiopia and in India, but was very quickly sent away, since he was not a holy or sacred person, nor truly a philosopher, but possessed a great deal of pollution from his sorcery.[A] ⁶The Julians and Ostaneses and Simons and such a coterie of wicked men, of what might someone now accuse them?[B] To merely recall them is to be filled with pollution!

⁷As for a man who is holy, living a well-ordered life suited to God, out of prayer alone, a few words, and not many tears he brings about very easily and handily what he wants God to make happen for him.

⁸Of this sort was Elijah, who uttered certain small things and proffered some rustic phrases, yet accomplished great things.

[A]. Apollonius was a first-century philosopher and wonderworker memorialized in Philostratus's *Life of Apollonius of Tyana* in the third century. In that work Apollonius was welcomed among the Indian sages but himself found the Gymnosophists of Ethiopia less admirable.

[B]. The author refers to three famous magicians: Julian, the author of the "Chaldean Oracles"; Ostanes, the Persian *magos* supposedly responsible for introducing the magical arts to Greece and Rome; and Simon Magus, first known in the canonical Acts and amplified by later Christian writers into the first archheretic.

THE LIFE OF THECLA

And certainly he kept performing entirely great deeds, the one who merely by saying, "As the Lord lives, before whom I have stood this day, there will be rain on the land only if it is through my mouth" closed up the skies for three whole years and six months and kept it cloudless, and then opened it up again and made it produce rain when it seemed right to him.

[margin: 1 Kgs 17:1; 18:41–45; cf. Jas 5:17–18]

⁹Of this sort was Moses, who just from prayer and raising up his holy hands to the sky defeated an entire people in battle (that is the Amalekites). And again in this way he ordered a sea, so great and unstable an element, to be its opposite—for he divided it for the passage of the people, and brought it together again—and he accomplished this too by prayer.

[margin: Exod 17:11]

[margin: Exod 14]

¹⁰Of this sort was Peter, who just through prayer and a barbarian-sounding voice[A] also raised the dead; and gates that were secured and very well locked he threw open and he dissolved the chains which enclosed him; ¹¹and Simon, that notorious *magos*, who seemed to be flying into heaven, he drew him back down and flung him at last down onto the earth from that ethereal sphere. Now Rome, the greatest and imperial city, was witness to this miracle.

[margin: Acts 9:40; 12:10]

[margin: Acts Pet. 32; Acts. Pet. Paul 77]

¹²Of this sort was Paul, who shook an entire prison from its depths and nearly brought it down, who raised Eutychus from the dead, and who blinded Elymas, a person renowned for sorcery.

[margin: Acts 16:26; 20:9–10; 13:8–11]

¹³So too through similar types of prayers and words was Thecla able to overcome fire and lions and bulls and sea-creatures! So then she responded and said to the judge:

THECLA: DEFENSE BEFORE THE GOVERNOR

¹⁴"I am as you see: a woman, a young girl, a stranger, and alone. God is my champion and my patron, and his only-begotten Son, who from long ago has existed and co-existed and been forever with his Father, but has now appeared on the earth and been proclaimed through many others and through my own teacher,

---

A. The author seems to be conflating Peter's phrase in Acts 9:40—"Tabitha, get up," where Tabitha is the name of the disciple also known in Greek as Dorcas—with the gospel scene on which it is modeled: Jesus' saying in Mark 5:41 "*Talitha kum*" which (as Mark glosses) is Aramaic for "little girl, get up."

Paul. ¹⁵So then, having confidence and faith in this Jesus, I prevailed over the many fearsome beasts of Alexander and indeed over the tyranny and unholiness of that nobleman Alexander. Everyone who genuinely has confidence and faith in him will come upon gifts equal to or even greater than mine. ¹⁶*For he is*," she said—it would probably be better to add nothing to the very words the martyr used, for they were more sublime and theological than you find in women's understanding[A]— "*he is*," she said, "*the only touchstone of salvation and the realization of immortal life, furthermore the refuge of the distressed and the relief of the afflicted, the shelter of the despairing. And, to put it quite simply,*" she said, "*whoever does not have faith in him will not live but will die forever.*" cf. John 11:26

Thecla Is Set Free

Acts Thec. 38

23 ¹When the martyr said these things, the governor was amazed at the intensity and manliness of the girl, and at the dignified and philosophical tenor of her words; more out of respect than pity, and amazement rather than mercy, he ordered that she be dressed in suitable clothing and that she receive ornament fitting for a reverent and temperate woman. ²When the clothing was brought to her, and the governor in his own voice invited her to make use of the clothing, the virgin received his words with pleasure and in response said:

THECLA: THANKS TO GOD AND THE GOVERNOR

³"God assisted me when I was stripped naked and presented to the beasts as food; he granted me the shelter of his light and covered me in his honor when I was in a dishonorable moment and condition; you, who at present have power on earth and have dressed me in these clothes, at the moment of the resurrection and kingdom may he clothe you in unceasing and unending

---

A. As the author indicates, he is once more citing directly from the *Acts*, flagged additionally by the repetition of "she said" (φησί, *phēsi*).

salvation and, instead of these corruptible and perishable things, may he reward you with his immortal and eternal gifts."

⁴When Thecla had prayed such things, the governor, wanting to make her dazzle even more gloriously and splendidly, in his own voice and with such words, declared to the Antiochene public:

GOVERNOR: PRAISE OF THECLA

⁵"Men of Antioch:[A] what Alexander said and asserts against this girl, it seems, is neither reliable nor true. We should not let his anger adjudicate her way and manner of life, but instead the great marvel of the deeds just now accomplished concerning her own self. We have all observed them in common; these matters are numerous and wondrous and truly worthy of a sign from God. ⁶That she was cast out to so many and such harmful beasts—such that it often caused a great shudder because of them for those of us seated above and watching—and that she came back safe and sound, how could it not be clear even to the very stupid that some god from heaven truly shields her and fights for her, on account of her life of temperance, of modesty and dignity befitting well-born girls? ⁷You saw just now how she stood among the beasts, reached out her hands to heaven, and drew down from there aid against the beasts—this more than anything stunned me into a daze and great wonder—and how some of the beasts didn't approach her at all, while others as they approached instead were playing the part of some fearful supplicant, lying down and cuddling at the girl's feet, and those who rushed to harm her were destroyed by their own fellow beasts. ⁸And when that great cry and lamentation advanced into the very upper air, the animal spectacle was filled with it, the whole city was filled with it, as such a great and miraculous and superior wonder, contrary to human nature, had taken place. ⁹Why shouldn't we send her forth with fitting praise, as dignified, as temperate, and as one who is respectably enslaved to God, who has become the cause of divine and miraculous wonders in this city, such that she has taught the women among us not to

---

A. The author expands a single sentence from the governor freeing Thecla in *Acts* into this long and elaborate speech of praise.

consider anything more honorable than temperance, even if it were necessary to face off against fire or sword or beasts? ¹⁰Have no more fear, my girl! You will no longer deal with any evil trial! For indeed should we wish to inflict one upon you, you would suffer no harm, since you have been armed with invincible and adamantine weapons. But go forth to those whom you desire and wherever you wish: only establish your god as kindly and favorable to us, whoever he is!"

Thecla and Tryphaena Are Reunited Acts Thec. 39

24 ¹When the public heard these things, they applauded and sang out in hymns full of praise for God.^A Many of the women hurried to Tryphaena; they brought the good news of Thecla's deliverance to her—how she was set free from the beasts and was hastening on to her. ²As a result, when she heard these things, Tryphaena was reanimated, so to speak, and brought back to life again and wondered when and where she would see Thecla. When she did see her, she clung to her and embraced her and then finally let loose tears of delight over her; as she welcomed her she said to her:

TRYPHAENA: THANKS TO THECLA

³"My child, I have rejoiced at seeing you so unexpectedly saved and rescued from the trial of so many evils. I have rejoiced even more that not only were you saved against all hope, but that I have seen the proof of the words concerning the resurrection, which you spoke so often to me, come to pass in you first of all. ⁴That you so clearly escaped death and an end already made plain has produced in me a sufficient and very confident assurance! As a result I have also been persuaded about my only beloved daughter Falconilla, that what was requested has truly come to pass through your prayer. ⁵But come now! Become the heir of all that I have! For if you have not begrudged me the

---

A. Once more, the author omits an instance of direct speech by the Antiochene women that appears in the *Acts*.

good things which are in heaven, shall I jealously withhold from you these earthly and perishable things? Now come and assume the status of Falconilla for me also in the succession of property: for I think this would please her."

⁶As Tryphaena said these things, all the women rushed together to her house and they were accomplishing nothing apart from rejoicing and discussing God. As a result Tryphaena's home was a church rather than a dwelling. ⁷Beginning her instruction from this home, so to speak, the martyr by her discourse of faith made Tryphaena one of her own and not a few of those who were in service to Tryphaena, the ranks of enslaved boys and girls, and she enlisted them in Christ's army through the seal.ᴬ

cf. 2 Tim 2:4

Acts Thec. 40

Thecla and Paul Are Reunited

25 ¹Although there was such excessive joy over Thecla herself, and Tryphaena was completely agape at her with longing and constantly inflamed, and the city too possessed the greatest glory over her, nevertheless the martyr was stupefied by Paul and she had nothing else to say except: "Paul" and "Where is Paul?" and "Who will let me know where he is, the one whom Christ has given to me as a governor and guide to his way of life and to the faith?" ²For although she was already well-known and famous from her wondrous deeds, she did not in the end disregard her teacher: she was instead still very beholden to him, understanding that these things especially accrued to her from him: faith, life, miracles and, greater and more outstanding, being completely attached and joined together to Christ. For once one has provided the seed one must count on what comes after.

³While she was greatly fretting and diligently inquiring, she was informed that Paul was in Myra (that is the capital city of Lycia). Learning this, and without any delay, she left Antioch, putting on again something more manly to wear in order to conceal with her outfit the shining bloom of her youth—for no misfortunes of this sort were able to bedim or obscure her beauty, which instead was made more honorable and conspicuous by the beauty of her

---

A. While Thecla's desire to baptize herself was attenuated above, here she unequivocally baptizes members of Tryphaena's household.

The Life of Thecla

soul. ⁴She made for the city of Myra, separated from Antioch by no little sea and land. Longing for the teacher cut it short for her and for those following along in her longing: they were the young men and women enslaved to Tryphaena.

⁵As she came into the city of Myra, she found Paul himself doing his usual favorite things: teaching, exhorting, admonishing, instructing through his discourse about faith. Many Lycian men and women were attending to this teaching of Paul's. ⁶As she suddenly came near and appeared she filled all of them with wonder and speechlessness, and Paul with fear: for the previous misfortunes moved him to suspicion of other bad things. ⁷So then drawing her away at some distance from the sight of the crowd and those present—so that no one, wounded by her beauty, might become once more the cause of more serious matters—he asked her about everything, and asked her again. ⁸As he heard about each one of the things that happened to her in Antioch, he was amazed at the virgin for her endurance, her perseverance, and her courage, but he was amazed at God for his splendid assistance concerning her and he exulted over Tryphaena, as she also contributed so much to the martyr in her contest. With great joy at these words, as it seems, in reply she said to Paul:ᴬ

Thecla Rejoices with Paul   *Acts Thec. 41*

THECLA: ON PAUL'S TEACHING

26 ¹"My teacher, the things I have acquired through you and through your teaching are numerous and surpass description.

²"For through you I have come to know God, the King of all, and his Son, the Only-begotten who reigns with the Father and is Creator of all, and the Holy Spirit who reigns with the Father and the Son and sanctifies and perfects all, a consubstantial Trinity of equal honor and status.

³"Through you I have come to know the equal status, the undifferentiation, and the same glory of the divinity in Trinity.

A. In the *Acts*, Thecla merely announces her baptized state to Paul and her intention to return to Iconium; the author expands this simple declaration into a fulsome theological confession.

The Life of Thecla

⁴"Through you I have come to know the ineffability, the inaccessibility, the immutability, the incomprehensibility of the power in Trinity.

⁵"Through you I have come to know that the consubstantial Trinity is in heaven and beyond the highest heaven, and on the earth and below the earth, and everywhere and over and around all things.

⁶"Through you I have come to know that the consubstantial Trinity is in nature and condition intelligible and sensible, seen and unseen, and rational and irrational.

⁷"Through you I have come to know that the consubstantial Trinity is in each and in all and throughout all, and it fills all and is filled by all.

⁸"Through you I have come to know that the consubstantial Trinity is not grasped by a mind nor spoken in a word nor observed by eyes nor discernible to the ear nor touched by a hand but observed by faith and worship alone.

⁹"Through you I have come to know that the consubstantial Trinity is all-powerful, all-observant, all-embracing, without beginning, uncreated, beyond time, without end, invincible.

¹⁰"Yet still further through you I have come to know the great mystery, which is beyond every rational and intelligible notion, of the birth of the Only-begotten according to flesh.

¹¹"Through you I have come to know the power of the wonders, the miracles, and the teachings of Christ.

¹²"Through you I have come to know the cause and the benefit of the cross, the death, the resurrection, and the assumption of Christ into heaven.

¹³"Through you I have come to know how the consummation, the resurrection, the judgment, the second coming of Christ are free of lies and deception.

¹⁴"Through you I have come to know that the kingdom in heaven and the unending blessedness of the saints is without mixture and without end.

¹⁵"Through you I have come to know that hell, the fire, the river of flame,^A the terrors and punishments and tortures in Death are boundless and impartial.

A. On the author's highly classicizing underworld vocabulary, see the

The Life of Thecla

[16]"Through you I have come to know the delight of paradise, the rest free from toil, the banquet free from effort that sets itself.

[17]"Through you I have come to know the grace and power of the divine washing and baptism by word and experience.

[18]"Through you I have learned the grace of chastity and virginity.

"Through you I have learned the usefulness of abstinence and perseverance.

"Through you I have learned the profit of prayer, of fasting, of charity.

[19]"Through you I have learned about the crowns reserved for the sufferings on behalf of Christ and because of Christ, and the struggles and pains and, quite simply, the prizes and rewards of complete piety and a way of life according to Christ reserved for those who love him.

[20]"These things then have accrued to me through you and through your teaching, and there are a great many more besides. If something is left out from what I've said, once you've added it on release me right away. For already the time has come for me to leave and to make for my own city, Iconium. [21]As for you, do not stop praying and beseeching on my behalf, so that I might finish the course of piety to the end without impediment or dishonor, and that I might make for the Kingdom of Heaven and receive Christ as my king and my bridegroom, because of whom I have suffered these things, and perhaps I shall suffer again and I shall be victorious again. [22]But you alone, my teacher, do not ever cease praying and pleading on behalf of me, your daughter. For you have begotten me in your bonds according to Christ."

In response to these things Paul said:

PAUL: PRAISE OF THECLA

[23]"Now you have done well in all these things, virgin, and through all of them the might of the faith has accrued to you; already you have prevailed in the apostolic toils and races, such that you now lack nothing for the apostleship and succession of the divine

---

introduction, p. 35.

preaching.^A^ So go and teach the word, and finish the gospel-spreading race, and share my eagerness on behalf of Christ. ²⁴This is why Christ has chosen you through me: so that he might acquire you for the apostleship, and so that he might put in your hands some of those cities which have not yet been catechized. For it is necessary for you to multiply the talents of gold."

cf. Matt 25:14–29

²⁵When Paul had said such things, the martyr left behind for Paul the property that had been given to her from Tryphaena—there was a lot of gold and expensive clothing—for the care of the poor; responding to these things with "Commend me to Christ!" she took to the road to Iconium.

Acts Thec. 42–43

Thecla Returns to Iconium and Journeys on to Seleucia

27 ¹When she finished the journey and was in the town, she avoided her mother and family and even her home and headed for Onesiphorus's house, in remembrance and longing for the place where first a ray of light began to shine on her, I mean the faith and knowledge of God. ²Looking at the place where Paul was sitting and teaching at that time, she fell face-down on it and kissed and watered the ground with her tears; she declared with such words as these:

THECLA: PRAISE TO GOD

³"God," she said, "who became known to me here and there through the good graces of your Only-begotten Son and through the teaching of Paul; God," she said, "who found me worthy of the contest through fire and bonds and beasts; ⁴God," she said, "who granted to me out of your light a shield when I was naked, who granted me the seal and the divine bath, who found me worthy to see Paul again, so that I might once more be strengthened by words from him, who guided me back to this city of mine and to this salvific home which is beloved to me: ⁵allow me, even in all things afterward, to do what is pleasing to you and to your Son,

---

A. Paul confirms Thecla's status as an apostle.

and never to stop fighting on behalf of the piety and faith which has become clear to me from you, even if every day it should be necessary for me to encounter fire and beasts and bonds and jails. ⁶As for me, every death and danger on behalf of piety is preferable to the delight and banquet in paradise: that I might only appear worthy to suffer because of you and for you always!"

⁷So having said these things, and then having discussed a few things with her mother Theocleia about faith and conduct according to Christ (for Thamyris had already died),^A she hurried off for Seleucia. ⁸This is a city which lies at the outskirts of the territory of Oriens, presiding and having preeminence over every city of Isauria, abutting a sea and neighboring a river. The name of the river is Calycadnus; it comes down from the inland regions of Cetis and passes through numerous regions and cities. ⁹On its journey toward us it also incorporates other rivers from their respective regions and locations and becomes that which we ultimately see. It ends at us and at the neighboring sea, which stretches to the East and to the South and separates us from Cyprus. ¹⁰The city is wonderful and most elegant, being of such a size that it lacks no grace in its proportion. She is so splendid and charming that she exceeds most but is the equal of others; she rivals Tarsus for her beauty, on account of her boundaries and disposition, and her temperate climate, abundance of fruits, lavishness of wares, readiness of waters, grace of baths, illustriousness of those in office, eloquence of arts, brilliance of its public, fluency of its orators, and the grandeur of those in military uniform. ¹¹On one point alone is she inferior in her great rivalry and in a way slightly subordinate and forgoing her precedence to that other place:^B that the other is the homeland and city of the great Paul, from whom it became possible for us to have the holy virgin.

¹²So then: having arrived at this city and finding it pleasing, she made for the neighboring hill which rose up to the south and made a dwelling-place for herself, like Elijah on Carmel or like John in the wilderness. ¹³She fortified herself against the demon

---

A. The author eschews an opportunity to put an invented speech in Thecla's mouth here, even though the *Acts* reports her words to her mother.

B. That is, to Tarsus.

The Life of Thecla

Sarpedon,^A who occupied a ridge over the sea and deceived many and led them astray from the faith through various deceptions and fraudulent oracles. ^14 She also fortified herself against the lofty and warlike demon Athena, who like a vulture (according *Homer, Il. 7.59* to Homer) perhaps even now is occupying the tower named for her; to the weavers dwelling in that area and to the foolish little people she cries out and brandishes her grimy and fringed aegis, so that we might make a little fun of all those people there who, in an Athenian manner, dwell on that acropolis and revere Pallas.^B

The End of Thecla's Life

28 ^1 Having preached the good news of the saving word and *cf. 2 Tim 2:4* catechized and sealed and enlisted many in Christ's army, and having performed an even greater number of miracles—like Peter in Antioch and greatest Rome, Paul in Athens and among all the nations, John the greatest theologian in Ephesus—and especially having drawn in everyone to the faith through these miracles, ^2 she by no means died, as the fulsome and more reliable story goes, but she sunk down while still living and went down into the earth, as it was pleasing to God to separate and split open for her that ground in the place where the divine and holy and liturgical table was fixed, set up in a round colonnade shining with silver; ^3 and for every suffering and every illness she sends forth streams of cures from that very spot, as if from some fountain of virginal grace gushing forth cures from there for those who ask and beg. As a result it is a place of healing for all people, and is established as a common site of propitiation for all the earth. ^4 You might never find her shrine (or indeed, city, for

---

A. In *Miracle 1*, which gives a fuller account of Thecla's expulsion of Sarpedon, the author provides an alternative history for this heroic age figure: rather than the son of Europa, who died in the Trojan War, he is the brother of Europa who died near Seleucia while searching for her and "took the name of a demon, and the reputation of an oracle and prophet" (Dagron, *Vie et miracles*, 290; see also Dagron's discussion on pp. 86–87).

B. Although *Miracle 2* recounts Thecla's ousting of the local version of Athena (Dagron, *Vie et miracles*, 292), she still seems to be venerated by some locals in the author's own time on the citadel named for her (called here an "acropolis"). "Pallas" is a classical name for Athena.

it at last has been built up into a city with respect to its form, its bustle, and its beauty) without locals or foreigners, with everyone streaming into it from everywhere: some only for honor and prayer, eager to offer up and dedicate something of their own to her; others for treatment and assistance from the illnesses and pains and even demons oppressing them.

⁵I shall produce a memorial of these through another labor and book, if God wills it and the virgin helps me.^A For we need a great deal of labor and time for the collection and more accurate recounting of the miracles accomplished by her, always and even until now, of which not a few of those miracles have been performed by her for me. ⁶No one who has ever been ignored when begging for treatment or release from ailments, no one who has been deceived by suspicious and dubious statements (such as those from the most excellent demons and oracles!), no one who has failed to find any treatment at all has left disparaging her great reputation. ⁷Everyone, in every way, receiving something of what they request or need, thus departs singing her praises, thanking her, blessing her, such that they reckon they have found miracles and cures greater than were rumored and hoped for. ⁸O virgin and martyr and apostle, may it be possible for us—the one who ordered me (I mean that holy man who is your ward)^B and myself, who was persuaded after having brought forth long ago this desire to produce in some form the narrative of your deeds—to find you always propitious and kindly, advocating on our behalf for what is fitting before God, being always present with us, and guarding us, and providing for us through yourself what is lawful for you to provide, and procuring for us through God what is most noble and most excellent, and useful, and favorable to you, virgin, and to Christ our God who provides, to whom all glory is fitting, all honor and might, now and forever and for eternity. Amen.

   A. The author signals his intention again to write a companion book of *Miracles*, which he has apparently not yet begun.

   B. Unnamed here, this "ward" is Achaius whom the author mentions in his preface.

Bibliography

Texts and Translations

Cunningham, Mary B., ed. and trans. "Basil of Seleucia's Homily on Lazarus: A New Edition (*BHG* 2225)." *AnBoll* 104 (1986) 161–84.

Dagron, Gilbert, ed. and trans. *Vie et miracles de Sainte Thècle: Text grec, traduction et commentaire*. Subsidia Hagiographica 62. Brussels: Société des Bollandistes, 1978. (pp. 168–282)

Egeria. *Itinerary*. Translated by John Wilkinson. 3rd ed. Warminster: Aris & Phillips, 1999.

Elliott, J. K., trans. *The Apocryphal New Testament*. Oxford: Clarendon, 1993 (*Acts of Thecla*, pp. 364–72).

Epiphanius of Cyprus. *Panarion*. Translated by Frank Williams. 2 vols. NHMS 63 & 79. Leiden: Brill, 2009, 2013.

Evagrius Scholasticus. *Ecclesiastical History*. Translated by Michael Whitby. Translated Texts for Historians 33. Liverpool: Liverpool University Press, 2000.

Gregory of Nazianzus. *Concerning His Own Life*. Translated by Denis Molaise Meehan, Thomas P. Halton, and Denis Molaise Meehan. FC 75. Washington, DC: Catholic University of America Press, 2010.

Honey, Linda Ann. "Thekla: Text and Context with a First English Translation of the *Miracles*." PhD diss., University of Calgary, 2008. (translation, pp. 362–446)

Johnson, Scott Fitzgerald. "Miracles of Thecla." In *Miracle Tales from Byzantium*, translated by Alice-Mary Talbot and Scott Fitzgerald Johnson, 1–201. Dumbarton Oaks Medieval Library 12. Cambridge: Harvard University Press, 2012. (Greek text and English translation)

Severus of Antioch. *Cathedral Homilies*. Syriac text and French translation in *Les homélies cathédrales de Sévère d'Antioche*. Edited by Maurice Brière. PO 25.1. Paris: Firmin-Didot, 1943.

Tertullian. *On Baptism*. Edited and translated by Ernest Evans (as *Tertullian's Homily on Baptism*). London: SPCK, 1964.

Themistius. *Oration* 8. Translated by David Moncur in *The Goths in the Fourth Century*, edited by Peter Heather and John Matthews, 24–33. Translated Texts for Historians. Liverpool: Liverpool University Press, 1991.

Theodoret of Cyrus. *Religious History*. Translated by R. M. Price as *A History of the Monks of Syria*. Cistercian Studies 88. Kalamazoo, MI: Cistercian, 1985.

BIBLIOGRAPHY

Studies and Other Works Cited

Andrious, Rosie. *Thecla: Body Politics and Masculine Rhetoric*. LNTS 596. London: T. & T. Clark, 2020.

Barrier, Jeremy W. *The Acts of Paul and Thecla: A Critical Introduction and Commentary*. WUNT 2/270. Tübingen: Mohr Siebeck, 2009.

———. "A Cainite Invocation of Thecla? The Reception of the *Acts of Paul* in North Africa as Exemplified in Tertullian's *de Baptismo*." In *Thecla and Medieval Sainthood: The Acts of Paul and Thecla in Eastern and Western Hagiography*, edited by Ghazzal Dabiri and Flavia Ruani, 35–60. Cambridge: Cambridge University Press, 2022.

———. "Paul and Thecla, Acts of." In *Brill Encyclopedia of Early Christianity Online*, edited by David G. Hunter, Paul J. J. van Geest, and Bert Jan Lietaert Peerbolte. 2018. Online: http://dx.doi.org/10.1163/2589-7993_EECO_SIM_00002591.

Berkowitz, Beth A. *Execution and Invention: Death Penalty Discourse in Early Rabbinic and Christian Cultures*. New York: Oxford University Press, 2006.

Betancourt, Roland. *Byzantine Intersectionality: Sexuality, Race, and Gender in the Middle Ages*. Princeton: Princeton University Press, 2020.

Brock, Sebastian P. "Poetry and Hymnography (3): Syriac." In *The Oxford Handbook of Early Christian Studies*, edited by Susan Ashbrook Harvey and David G. Hunter, 657–71. Oxford: Oxford University Press, 2009.

Burns, Dylan M. "Astrological Determinism, Free Will, and Desire according to Thecla (St. Methodius, *Symposium* 8.15–16)." In *Women and Knowledge in Early Christianity*, edited by Ulla Tervahauta, Ivan Miroshnikov, Outi Lehtippu, and Ismo Dunderberg, 206–20. VCSup 144. Leiden: Brill, 2017.

Burris, Catherine. "The Reception of the Acts of Thecla in Syriac Christianity: Translation, Collection, and Reception." PhD diss., University of North Carolina, 2010.

Burrus, Virginia. *Chastity as Autonomy: Women in the Stories of the Apocryphal Acts*. Studies in Women and Religion 23. Lewiston, NY: Mellen, 1987.

———. "Mimicking Virgins: Colonial Ambivalence and the Ancient Romance." *Arethusa* 38 (2005) 49–88.

Castelli, Elizabeth. *Martyrdom and Memory: Early Christian Culture Making*. New York: Columbia University Press, 2004.

Chin, C. Michael. *Grammar and Christianity in the Late Roman World*. Divinations. Philadelphia: University of Pennsylvania Press, 2008.

Clark, Elizabeth A. *Reading Renunciation: Asceticism and Scripture in Early Christianity*. Princeton: Princeton University Press, 1999.

Cooper, Kate. *The Virgin and the Bride: Idealized Womanhood in Late Antiquity*. Cambridge: Harvard University Press, 1996.

Dabiri, Ghazzal, and Flavia Ruani, eds. *Thecla and Medieval Sainthood: The Acts of Paul and Thecla in Eastern and Western Hagiography*. Cambridge: Cambridge University Press, 2022.

Dagron, Gilbert. "L'auteur des 'Actes' et de 'Miracles' de Sainte Thècle." *AnBoll* 92 (1974) 5–11.

Davies, Stevan L. *The Revolt of the Widows: The Social World of the Apocryphal Acts*. Carbondale: Southern Illinois University Press, 1980.

Davis, Stephen J. "Crossed Texts, Crossed Sex: Intertextuality and Gender in Early Christian Legends of Holy Women Disguised as Men." *JECS* 10 (2002) 1–36.

Bibliography

———. *The Cult of Saint Thecla: A Tradition of Women's Piety in Late Antiquity*. OECS. Oxford: Oxford University Press, 2001.

———. "Thecla." In *The Encyclopedia of Ancient History*. Edited by Roger S. Bagnall et al., 6661–63. London: Blackwell, 2013.

Eastman, David L. *The Ancient Martyrdom Accounts of Peter and Paul*. WGRW 39. Atlanta: Society of Biblical Literature, 2015.

Eyl, Jennifer. "Apocryphal Acts of the Apostles." In *The Oxford Handbook of New Testament, Gender, and Sexuality*, edited by Benjamin H. Dunning, 387–404. Oxford Handbooks. Oxford: Oxford University Press, 2019.

Frank, Georgia. "Crowds and Collective Affect in Romanos's Biblical Retellings." In *The Garb of Being: Embodiment and the Pursuit of Holiness in Late Ancient Christianity*, edited by Georgia Frank, Susan R. Holman, and Andrew Jacobs, 169–90. New York: Fordham University Press, 2019.

Gager, John. *Curse Tablets and Binding Spells from the Ancient World*. New York: Oxford University Press, 1992.

Hayne, Léonie. "Thecla and the Church Fathers." VC 48 (1994) 209–18.

Herzfeld, Ernst, and Samuel Guyer. *Meriamlik und Korykos: Zwei christliche Ruinenstätte des Rauhen Kilikiens*. MAMA 2. Manchester: Manchester University Press, 1930.

Hill, Stephen. *The Early Byzantine Churches of Cilicia and Isauria*. Birmingham Byzantine and Ottoman Monographs 1. Ashgate: Variorum, 1996.

Hillner, Julia. *Prison, Punishment, and Penance in Late Antiquity*. Cambridge: Cambridge University Press, 2015.

Hylen, Susan E. "The 'Domestication' of Saint Thecla: Characterization of Thecla in the *Life and Miracles of Saint Thecla*." JFSR 30.2 (2014) 5–21.

———. *A Modest Apostle: Thecla and the History of Women in the Early Church*. Oxford: Oxford University Press, 2015.

Jansen, Katherine Ludwig. "Maria Magdalena: Apostolorum Apostola." In *Women Preachers and Prophets through Two Millennia of Christianity*, edited by Beverly Mayne Kienzle and Pamela J. Walker, 57–96. Berkeley: University of California Press, 1998.

Johnson, Scott Fitzgerald. *The Life and Miracles of Thekla: A Literary Study*. Hellenic Studies Series 13. Cambridge: Center for Hellenic Studies/Harvard University Press, 2006.

Kaestli, Jean-Daniel, and Willy Rordorf. "La fin de la vie de Thècle dans les manuscrits des *Actes de Paul et Thècle*: Édition des textes additionels." Apocrypha 25 (2014) 9–101.

Kateusz, Ally. *Mary and Early Christian Women: Hidden Leadership*. New York: Palgrave Macmillan, 2019.

Kensky, Meira. "Ephesus, *Loca Sancta*: The Acts of Timothy and Religious Travel in Late Antiquity." In *The Narrative Self in Late Antiquity: Essays in Honor of Judith Perkins*, edited by Janet E. Spittler, 91–119. Writings from the Greco-Roman World Supplements 15. Atlanta: SBL Press, 2019.

Klauck, Hans-Josef. *The Apocryphal Acts of the Apostles: An Introduction*. Translated by Brian McNeil. Waco: Baylor University Press, 2008.

Kraemer, Ross Shepard. "Thecla." In *The Oxford Handbook of New Testament, Gender, and Sexuality*, edited by Benjamin H. Dunning, 485–502. Oxford Handbooks. Oxford: Oxford University Press, 2019.

Krautheimer, Richard. *Three Christian Capitals: Topography and Politics*. Berkeley: University of California Press, 1983.

Bibliography

Kristensen, Troels Myrup. "Landscape, Space, and Presence in the Cult of Thekla at Meriamlik." *JECS* 24 (2016) 229–63.

Krueger, Derek. *Writing and Holiness: The Practice of Authorship in the Early Christian East*. Divinations. Philadelphia: University of Pennsylvania Press, 2004.

Lavalle Norman, Dawn. *The Aesthetics of Hope in Late Greek Imperial Literature: Methodius of Olympus' Symposium and the Crisis of the Third Century*. Greek Culture in the Roman World. Cambridge: Cambridge University Press, 2019.

Lieber, Laura Suzanne. "On the Road with the Mater Dolorosa: An Exploration of Mother-Son Discourse Performance." *JECS* 24 (2016) 265–91.

Ludlow, Morwenna. *Art, Craft, and Theology in Fourth-Century Christian Authors*. Oxford: Oxford University Press, 2020.

MacDonald, Dennis R. *The Legend and the Apostle: The Battle for Paul in Story and Canon*. Philadelphia: Westminster, 1983.

MacDonald, Dennis R., and Andrew D. Scrimgeour. "Pseudo-Chrysostom's Panegyric to Thecla: The Heroine of the *Acts of Paul* in Homily and Art." *Semeia* 38 (1986) 151–59.

Marincola, John. "Speeches in Classical Historiography." In *A Companion to Greek and Roman Historiography*, edited by John Marincola, 119–32. Blackwell Companions to the Ancient World: Literature and Culture. Malden, MA: Blackwell, 2007.

McGinn, Thomas A.J. *The Economy of Prostitution in the Roman World: A Study of Social History and the Brothel*. Ann Arbor: University of Michigan Press, 2004.

Muehlberger, Ellen. *Moment of Reckoning: Imagined Death and Its Consequences in Late Ancient Christianity*. Oxford: Oxford University Press, 2019.

Narro, Ángel. "Lo scontro tra formazione classica e pensiero cristiano. La vita e miracoli di santa Tecla." *Graeco-Latina Brunensia* 15 (2010) 127–38.

Nasrallah, Laura Salah. "Judgment, Justice, and Destruction: *Defixiones* and 1 Corinthians." *JBL* 140 (2021) 347–67.

Nauerth, Claudia, and Rudiger Warns. *Thekla: Ihre Bilder in der frühchristlichen Kunst*. Göttinger Orientforschungen, Veröffentlichungen des Sonderforschungsbereiches Orientalistik an der Georg-August-Universität Göttingen: II. Reihe, Studien zur spätantiken und frühchristlichen Kunst 3. Wiesbaden: Harrassowitz, 1981.

Patel, Shaily Shashikant. "Notes on Rehabilitating 'Magic' in the Study of Early Christian Literature." *Religion Compass* 15.10 (2021) 1–12. Online: https://compass.onlinelibrary.wiley.com/doi/abs/10.1111/rec3.12415.

Perkins, Judith. *The Suffering Self: Pain and Narrative Representation in the Early Christian Era*. London: Routledge, 1995.

Pillinger, Renate Johanna. "Thekla in the Cave of St. Paul at Ephesos." In *Religion in Ephesos Reconsidered: An Archaeology of Space, Structures, and Objects*, edited by Daniel Schowalter et al., 62–72. Novum Testamentum Supplements 177. Leiden: Brill, 2020.

Porter, Sarah F. "A Church and Its Charms: Space, Affect, and Affiliation in Late Fourth-Century Antioch." *Studies in Late Antiquity* 2021 (5) 639–77.

Rordorf, Willy. "Saint Thècle dans la tradition hagiographique occidentale." *Aug* 24 (1984) 73–81.

Smith, Yancy Warren. "Hippolytus' Commentary on the Song of Songs in Social and Critical Context." PhD diss., Brite Divinity School, 2009.

Spittler, Janet E. "Apostles, Apocrypha Acts of the." In *Brill Encyclopedia of Early Christianity Online*, edited by David G. Hunter et al. Leiden: Brill, 2018. Online: http://dx.doi.org/10.1163/2589-7993_EECO_SIM_00000242.

Bibliography

Thomas, Christine M. *The Acts of Peter, Gospel Literature, and the Ancient Novel: Rewriting the Past*. Oxford: Oxford University Press, 2003.

Van Pelt, Julie. "Thecla, the First Cross-Dresser? The *Acts of Paul and Thecla* and the Lives of Byzantine Transvestite Saints." In *Thecla and Medieval Sainthood: The* Acts of Paul and Thecla *in Eastern and Western Hagiography*, edited by Ghazzal Dabiri and Flavia Ruani, 197–232. Cambridge: Cambridge University Press, 2022.

Wendt, Heidi. *At the Temple Gates: The Religion of Freelance Experts in the Roman Empire*. Oxford: Oxford University Press, 2016.

Wuk, Michael. "Pragmatic Necessity over Scriptural Guidelines: Basil of Seleucia and the Swearing of Oaths at Later Roman Church Councils." *JECS* 30 (2022) 555–85.

Index of Ancient Sources

Hebrew Bible/Old Testament

Exodus
7–10	83
14	86
17:11	86

1 Kings
17:1	86
18:41–45	86

Job
1–2	60

Song of Songs
3:1–3	58

Isaiah
52:7	75
53:7	65

Daniel
3:17–27	81
3:21–27	67
6:17–24	81

New Testament

Matthew
4:8–10	60
13:30	69
19:10–12	46
25:14–29	94

Mark
8:34	60

Luke
1:30	43

John
1:14	45
11:26	87
12:24	69

Acts of the Apostles
1:1	43
7	43
8:32	65
9:40	86
11:26	71
12:10	86
13:6–12	31
13:8–11	86
14:1–5	43
16:26	86
20:9–10	86
22:3–4	43
23:29	57

Romans
1:20–28	56
6:3–4	82
10:15	75
16:1	24
16:3, 7	24

1 Corinthians
7:9	57
7:29	46
15:53	57

2 Corinthians
11:2	59

Index of Ancient Sources

Galatians
1:13–14   43
6:17   82

Colossians
4:14   3

1 Timothy
1:13   43

2 Timothy
1:6   3
1:15   3
1:16   44
2:3   61
2:4   90, 96
4:19   3, 44

Philemon
1:24   3

Hebrews
11:10   57

James
5:17–18   86

Pseudepigrapha

Acts of John
88   45

Acts of Peter
32   86

Acts of Philip
8:21   25
9:1   25

Acts of the Holy Apostles Peter and Paul
77   86

Acts of Thecla
1   43
2–4   44
3   53
5–6   45
7–10   32
7–8   46
9   48
10   49
11–14   50–51
13   52
15–16   52–53
16   53
17   55
18   57
19   62
20   63, 66
21–22   65
23–24   68, 69
25   26, 69
26   25, 69
27   71
28   74
29   75
30–31   77
32–33   79
34   29, 81
35–36   83
37   84
38   87
39   89
40   26, 90
41   34, 91
42–43   94
43   19

Greco-Roman Writings

Homer
Iliad
7.59   96
7.213   53

Themistius
Orations
8.114   58

Theodosian Code
16.6.27   27

Index of Ancient Sources

Early Christian Writings

Ps.-Basil of Seleucia
Miracles of Thecla

1	96
1–2	31
2	26, 96
4	24
7–8	12
10	34
11	6, 11
12	9–10, 12
17–19	10
31	10
37–40	11
41	12
44	12

Ps-Chrysostom
Panegyric to Thecla

	6

Ps-Clement of Rome
Homilies

1.4	35

Egeria
Itinerarium

23.4–6	7–8
23.5	5

Epiphanius
Panarion

77.27.7	5
78.16.7	6
79.5.2	6

Eusebius of Caesarea
De martyribus Palaestinae

10–11	6
20	6

Praeparatio evangelica

11.38	35

Evagrius
Ecclesiastical History

3.8	8

Gregory of Nazianzus
De vita sua

549	7

Epistulae

56	6
57	6
222	6
223	6

Orations

21	6

Gregory of Nyssa
In Canticum canticorum

14	6

De vita Macrinae

3.2	6

Hippolytus
In Canticum canticorum

25	25

Jerome
De viris illustribus

7	5

Methodius
Symposium

	6

Severus of Antioch
Homilia cathedralis

97	21, 73

Tertullian
De Baptismo

17	5

Theodoret
Religious History

29.7	8

www.ingramcontent.com/pod-product-compliance
Lightning Source LLC
Chambersburg PA
CBHW032234080426
42735CB00008B/857